LONDON'S BIG DAY
THE CORONATION 60 YEARS ON

LONDON'S BIG DAY
THE CORONATION 60 YEARS ON

DAVID LONG AND GAVIN WHITELAW

The History Press

First published 2013

The History Press
The Mill, Brimscombe Port
Stroud, Gloucestershire, GL5 2QG
www.thehistorypress.co.uk

British Library Cataloguing in Publication Data.
A catalogue record for this book is available from the British Library.

ISBN 978 0 7524 9714 3

Typesetting and origination by The History Press
Printed in Great Britain
Manufacturing managed by Jellyfish Solutions Ltd

Contents

INTRODUCTION

Sixty years on, arguably the most enduring memories of that cold wet June day in London are of grainy black and white images taken inside the lofty hushed portals of Westminster Abbey. This, after all, was the first time in history that the government and church authorities had agreed to allow such a sombre and important ceremony to be filmed for television and enjoyed by the wider public, and as a result those same images were always certain to cast a long shadow as they echoed down the years.

At the time the impact of the decision was indeed immense, with literally millions tuning in to view what was to be the most significant television event since John Logie Baird's first demonstration of his new 'televisor' back in the 1920s. Across Britain tens of thousands of households bought their first television sets expressly in order not to miss out on such an historic occasion. And on the day itself many thousands more, unable to afford what at this time was still a rare and major expense for most families, crowded into the homes of their better-heeled neighbours to enjoy the spectacle and pageantry of a truly splendid national occasion.

While much of what took place that day must have baffled foreigners, the excitement around the world was just as high, and with the coronation of the new sovereign of the United Kingdom the first such event anywhere in the world to be broadcast internationally, the larger overseas broadcasting organisations sent hundreds of their own commentators to London to provide bespoke coverage in more than thirty languages. Among them was Miss Jacqueline Bouvier of the *Washington Times-Herald*, who later that year married future president John F. Kennedy.

But perhaps best served was Canada, the Royal Air Force ordering its advanced new Canberra jet-bombers into the air so as to rush film across the Atlantic in record-breaking time to be shown by the Canadian Broadcasting Corporation with instant feeds to major US networks such as NBC and ABC[*].

The quality of this coverage, the attention to the tiniest detail of dress and protocol, and even more so the sheer novelty of having cameras present at such an event, nevertheless means that those same monochrome images are today the only ones that most of us ever see. How many know, for example, that there was a good deal of colour film shot on the day as well, and that a colour film of the Queen's Coronation, *A Queen is Crowned*, was afterwards narrated by the actor Laurence Olivier? (It was even nominated for an Oscar.) There was even some experimental 3D footage shot as well, although of course until the 1960s no home television sets at any price were able to show anything but ordinary black and white film – so that even now this other material is only very rarely seen.

Much harder to explain is that the photography and footage from outside Westminster Abbey is also now relatively unknown. Indeed much

---

[*] The operation, codenamed 'Pony Express', involved three Canberras lifting off at 1.30, 3.15 and 6.20 p.m. The flights took a little over five hours, so that at 4.15 p.m. local time a full 'telerecording' of the BBC's coverage was able to be broadcast by stations in Ottawa, Toronto and Montreal. Across the Atlantic more than two million homes tuned in to enjoy the show.

For weeks the eyes of the world were on London.

of this imagery – moving and still – is so rare that today it is all too easy to overlook just how big a show London put on for its new queen and for the world.

The weather may have been foul – so much worse than on the days of the two full dress rehearsals which had been conducted in late May – and 'Austerity Britain' meant Londoners and others were still very much caught up in the grip of the post-war, ration-book malaise, but against this there was a real determination in the country to make the most of the occasion. From the early morning, the area around the ancient Collegiate Church of St Peter at Westminster was thronging with respectful well-wishers hoping to glimpse members of the royal family and other dignitaries and to share in their joy.

Evidence of this can be seen in the many famous landmark buildings which were festooned with flags and bunting – looking down on Piccadilly Circus the figure of 'Eros' was temporarily housed in a gilded cage – and the immense grandstands which were erected at strategic points around the route along which the new sovereign would travel on her journeys to and from this most ancient of rituals. Also on the Mall, still London's only authentically ceremonial piece of town planning,

where giant illuminated arches and crowns were installed to lead the way to Buckingham Palace[*].

Happily the sight of all this can now be seen here in all its glory, in this hitherto private and unpublished collection of candid and informal colour photographs taken by members of the huge crowds which greeted the new sovereign when she emerged from the abbey. They show a London which is at once quite different to the London of today yet wholly familiar to anyone who walks the same streets sixty years on or views them from the top of a bus. By capturing the spirit of this great occasion, and the excitement which swept the country in the early summer of 1953, they more than anything convey the atmosphere and optimism and the real sense of history which was to greet Britain's New Elizabethan Age. The death of George VI may have been sudden and tragic, but the coronation of his daughter was to provide a tonic for a nation still bruised and battered by the war – and a reason to celebrate.

---

[*]   Linking the arches along the ceremonial route, and providing flashes of further colour, were long lines of standards mounted with golden crowns and hung with four scarlet banners bearing the royal monogram, EIIR.

Respectful crowds gather in the Mall for the rehearsal.

The weather was foul, but thousands came to see the pageantry and colour.

London was festooned with colours and decorative structures.

1

THE KING IS DEAD, LONG LIVE THE QUEEN

The historic proclamation signifying the continuity of a traditional hereditary monarchy is especially heavy with meaning when the deceased was loved and respected. That was certainly the case on 6 February 1952 when the death was announced of His Majesty King George VI of the United Kingdom of Great Britain and Northern Ireland, the last Emperor of India – and with it the accession of his daughter as Queen Elizabeth II.

Born at 2.40 a.m. at her maternal grandfather's Mayfair townhouse at 17 Bruton Street on 21 April 1926, it was only the abdication of her uncle a decade later that placed the young HRH Princess Elizabeth Alexandra Mary of York directly in line for the throne. And now, on the death of Britain's wartime king, as Queen Elizabeth II she became Sovereign Head of the Commonwealth and Queen Regnant of seven independent countries of the Commonwealth*.

The death was sudden but cannot have been entirely unexpected in establishment circles as the king had been suffering from a painful illness for a long time, and had undergone surgeries for cancer. At the time, however, few knew the full details of his condition, and certainly no one expected his death to come when it did. Just a week earlier he had visited the theatre with his wife, daughter and son-in-law, and shortly afterwards His Majesty had accompanied Princess Elizabeth and the Duke of Edinburgh to the airport, bidding them farewell as they set out on a lengthy trip through the Commonwealth on his behalf.

The king's death occurred while the princess was travelling in east Africa, specifically while she and Prince Philip were staying at the Treetops Hotel in Kenya. (It was afterwards observed by a lady-in-waiting, one of Lord Mountbatten's daughters, that Elizabeth had gone up the giant fig tree a princess and come down a queen.) Travelling to Sagana Lodge – a modest hunting lodge which had been given to the royal couple as a wedding present from the colony – it fell to Prince Philip to break the news to his wife who thus became the first British monarch since the Elector of Hanover, George I, to be outside the United Kingdom at the moment of succession.

In fact with the king's health evidently in decline since the previous year, Princess Elizabeth had already been undertaking many of his duties. Now she was to do so on her own behalf, and once she had decided on her regnal name – confirming that she would reign as Elizabeth – the news of her accession was proclaimed throughout the Commonwealth, and plans were made for the royal party to travel back to England.

It transpired that, having retired to his Sandringham estate for the winter break, a place where he could relax and go hunting, the king had spent his last evening doing a crossword puzzle while listening to his younger daughter Princess Margaret playing the piano. After tuning

---

* At the time of Her Majesty's accession the seven were the United Kingdom, Canada, Australia, New Zealand and South Africa, as well as Pakistan and Ceylon (now Sri Lanka). Since then the numbers have fluctuated as individual territories have gained independence or chosen to become republics, but at the time of writing Elizabeth II is the Sovereign Head of Jamaica, Barbados, the Bahamas, Grenada, Papua New Guinea, the Solomon Islands, Tuvalu, Saint Lucia, Saint Vincent and the Grenadines, Belize, Antigua and Barbuda and Saint Kitts and Nevis.

in to the BBC to hear news of Princess Elizabeth and Prince Philip, he had gone to bed, passing away peacefully in his sleep of a coronary thrombosis during the early hours.

The sad discovery of the king's death was made by his valet at 7.15 a.m., the news being first broken to his wife, now the Queen Mother, then his younger daughter, Princess Margaret, and his mother, Queen Mary, the new Queen Dowager. Calls were made to London after which officials from Buckingham Palace made the short crossing to Downing Street to inform the Prime Minister, Sir Winston Churchill. At 10.45 a.m. the aforementioned formal public announcement was made from Sandringham House, to the country and the Commonwealth, and a declaration in London signed by nearly 200 Privy Counsellors.

Dressed in mourning black, Her Majesty Queen Elizabeth II arrived on British soil during the afternoon of 7 February. Following a statement from Downing Street saying that, 'the Prime Minister feels that it would be in accordance with the wishes of the public that the return of the Queen to London should be as quiet as possible and that Her Majesty should be met only by those whose official positions make it appropriate for them to be present', there was no public gathering at Heathrow Airport. Instead Her Majesty's aeroplane, the DC-4M-4 Argonaut *Atalanta* of the British Overseas Airways Corporation, was met by Sir Winston Churchill, Mr Clement Atlee as Leader of the Opposition, HRH the Duke of Gloucester, and a number of members of her Privy Council. Conveyed by black Daimler car to Clarence House, she immediately approved arrangements for the king's funeral before being met by her grandmother, HM Queen Mary, who as custom required curtseyed and kissed the new queen's hand.

That evening the Prime Minister made a broadcast to the nation. The king, he said:

was greatly loved by all his peoples and respected as a man and as a prince far beyond the many realms over which he reigned. The simple dignity of his life, his manly virtues, his sense of duty – alike as ruler and servant of the vast spheres for which he bore responsibility – his gay charm and happy nature, his example as a husband and a father in his own family circles, his courage in peace or war – all of these were aspects of his character which won the glint of admiration, now here, now there, from the innumerable eyes whose gaze falls upon the throne.

Banners spoke for the nation – and the world.

Another statement was issued by the Archbishop of Canterbury, Dr Geoffrey Fisher, describing the late king as a grand leader of his people 'by reason of his courage, his simple humanity, his selfless regard for others, his single-minded devotion to duty. We thank God for his example.' Cardinal Griffin similarly, on behalf of Britain's Roman Catholics, sent a telegram mourning the sad loss 'of a great King'. By his selfless devotion to his duties, said the Cardinal, 'by his loving interest in the welfare of his peoples, by his courage in the face of illness and by his magnificent example of family life, King George VI had won a unique position in the hearts of his subjects.'

As reported by the BBC, it was Her Majesty who formally proclaimed herself queen, Head of the Commonwealth and Defender of the Faith, doing so from the sovereign's official London residence, St James's Palace, and in the presence of the Lords of the Council. These numbered 150 in total, and were joined by representatives from the Commonwealth, the Lord Mayor of London and other City of London dignitaries.

Before them all Elizabeth read an official proclamation, declaring her reign as Her Majesty Queen Elizabeth the Second. 'By the sudden death of my dear father,' she declared, 'I am called to assume the duties and responsibilities of sovereignty. My heart is too full for me to say more to you today than I shall always work, as my father did throughout his reign, to advance the happiness and prosperity of my peoples, spread as they are all the world over.'

Following the formality of this official Accession Declaration, the new queen held her first Privy Council meeting when her proclamation was signed by the Prime Minister, the Lord Chancellor and others present. It was then taken to the people, proclaimed at St James's Palace by the Garter King of Arms, who with a cavalry escort then proceeded to Charing Cross, where he read it once more, and then to Temple Bar, the entrance to the Square Mile, and to the Royal Exchange. Ceremonial gun salutes were fired from Hyde Park and the Tower of London, and the process repeated at Edinburgh, Windsor and York and – albeit with somewhat less pomp – at shire, town and guild halls around the country.

The body of the late king remained at Sandringham until the queen's arrival in Norfolk on 8 February. Once she had paid her respects to her father privately, his coffin, draped in the Royal Standard and accompanied by a bunch of white flowers from Queen Elizabeth the Queen Mother, was moved to St Mary Magdalene's Church where estate workers kept vigil, day and night, until 11 February. On that day a small cortege accompanied the coffin to the station where the royal train was waiting to return the king's body and the royal family to London.

In London, as was only to be expected, tens of thousands of people lined the streets to see the king's coffin pass on a gun carriage from Victoria station to Westminster Hall. The crowds were silent and their mood tangible, one of unbearable loss, of actual loneliness for some, and of profound sadness for many. Pulled by Windsor Greys and closely followed on foot by TRH the Dukes of Edinburgh and Gloucester, and then by the other members of the royal family, the procession made its way to the historic Palace of Westminster where the late king was to lie in state.

Once there members of the two Houses of Parliament, the Lords and the Commons, would assemble to pay their respects, as later would more than 300,000 loyal subjects, ordinary members of the public being admitted to the ancient, lofty and silent hall once the royal family and establishment grandees had withdrawn.

For Queen Mary it was to be the third time she had buried a son. Prince John, an invalid, had died when still a teenager and was buried on the Sandringham estate. HRH the Duke of Kent had been killed in a flying boat crash in Caithness in 1942, leaving three young children. And now, a frail old lady widowed sixteen years previously, the Dowager was mourning the loss of her beloved Bertie, King George VI. Notwithstanding the sadness of such a thing, the occasion provided an opportunity for a unique and historic portrait of three queens and three generations: Queen Mary, Queen Elizabeth the Queen Mother and Queen Elizabeth II, gathered together to see the passing of a son, a husband and a father.

The scene inside Westminster Hall was no less unique. Upon the dais the Royal Standard covered the king's coffin. Above this set on a cushion was the magnificent Imperial State Crown, set in turn with many diamonds and other precious stones, including Edward the Confessor's sapphire. Alongside this the King's Orb and the Royal Sceptre rested, the latter the very symbol of royal power and justice, while eight guards mounted a vigil over the coffin both day and night.

Preparations for the king's funeral were meanwhile well underway, in London and in Windsor, with heads of state from all over the world making their way to the capital. In Britain and in many countries abroad flags were flown at half-mast, and on the day itself, 15 February, an estimated two million people flooded onto the streets of London as, veiled and in mourning dress, the royal party arrived at Westminster Hall. (Queen Mary was sadly too frail to attend, and instead closely followed television images of her son's final journey from a room at Marlborough House.)

Elegant archways sprung up along the Mall.

Servicemen and women from all three branches lined the streets from the Palace of Westminster to Paddington station, where a platform had been prepared for the departure of the king's body for interment at Windsor Castle. At 9.30 a.m. exactly, a volley of gunfire, the first of fifty-six marking each year of the late king's life, coincided with the half-hour chime from Big Ben as eight officers emerged from Westminster Hall carrying the coffin. Placed on a gun carriage, and pulled by ninety-eight members of the Royal Marines (with a further forty behind to act as a brake) the late king was conveyed through London as part of a grand cortege accompanied by bands playing slow, sombre marches.

The queen, the Queen Mother, Princess Margaret and the late king's sister (Princess Mary, the Princess Royal) followed immediately behind in the Irish State Coach. Behind them came the four royal dukes of Edinburgh, Gloucester, Kent and Windsor – the latter in the uniform of an Admiral of the Fleet. The former King Edward VIII had made a rare return to Britain to pay homage to the younger brother who since the 1930s had shouldered the real burden of his own abdication.

Greatly swelled by further carriages and many more dignitaries marching on foot, the long, slow procession was to last almost three hours, finally arriving at Paddington station not much before 12.30 p.m. There, watched by the world, and in the presence of two queens and the two princesses, the king was about to leave London for the final time.

The sense of history was tangible.

In Windsor itself the mood was much as in London. In the shadow of the ancient fortress tens of thousands had flocked to the streets to see the cortege, to see the Royal Marines pulling the gun carriage with its sombre load. Once more the queen, the Queen Mother, the Princess Royal and Princess Margaret followed behind, this time in a Windsor Landau, and behind them came the same respectful line of royal dignitaries and statesmen slowly making their way towards the shrine of St George's Chapel.

At 2 p.m., as the cortege entered the castle gate, another fifty-six-gun salute sounded. Throughout Britain and the Commonwealth, a two-minute silence was observed as the gun carriage stopped in front of the chapel. Inside some 900 people assembled to hear a short, twenty-five-minute service given by the Dean of Windsor, after which the late king's body was lowered down into the royal vault.

Before it disappeared from view the Imperial State Crown, the King's Orb and the Royal Sceptre were removed from the coffin along with the Royal Standard. Each represented an important symbol of continuity, together standing for the unbreakable chain of sovereignty which now rested in the queen. Only her mother's white flowers remained with the coffin, and in the final act of this arcane, occasionally mysterious but deeply moving drama, the Garter King of Arms, looking straight at Her Majesty, loudly proclaimed what was to be a new era with the words 'God Save the Queen!'

Private and public buildings alike joined in the festivities.

Eager crowds flocked to the palace.

The world's press gathered in London.

Not since VE Day had the mood been so upbeat.

Equally thrilling for young and old.

For many it would have been their first trip to London.

2

A Thousand Years of History

The coronation of the new sovereign traditionally follows some months after his or her accession, a delay which allows for a period of mourning for the late monarch – both personal and official – as well as proving necessary to accommodate the enormous amount of preparation required in organising the complexities and ritual associated with such an important ceremony.

In Britain it is a ceremony which has remained essentially unchanged for at least 1,000 years. For more than 900 of these all but a very few coronations have taken place at Westminster Abbey in London, and been conducted by the Archbishop of Canterbury whose task this has almost always been since the Norman Conquest. There have indeed been very few exceptions to this pattern. William II was crowned at Winchester Cathedral in 1087, and Henry III at Gloucester in 1216; but in the former's case the Archbishop of Canterbury travelled to Winchester to officiate and four years after his first coronation Henry wisely chose to be crowned again back at Westminster.

While doubtless an occasion for great celebration, the actual crowning of a new monarch is nevertheless a deeply serious affair. A moment of the greatest and lasting significance for Crown and Country, it is one in which great symbolic value has always been vested. This was perhaps never better demonstrated than by the French invaders in 1066, when their ruler chose to be crowned on Christmas Day in Edward the Confessor's new Westminster Abbey – and with the doors locked to prevent any Saxons gaining entry.

Above all, the coronation is a very public moment, one which by its nature the moment of accession may not always be. On hearing of her own accession in 1558 Queen Elizabeth I had observed, 'This is the Lord's doing, and it is marvellous in our eyes', whereas five years earlier the tragic, ill-fated Lady Jane Grey had simply burst into tears after declaring that, 'The Crown is not my right, and it pleaseth me not'. In 1727 George II is also recorded as having expressed something approaching surprise, declaring in heavily accented English 'Dat is vun big lie!'

In many other cases, however, the new monarch's immediate reaction is simply not known: as consort Prince Philip has not surprisingly never publicly revealed any details about his wife's reaction to the news of her father's death. And while it seems quite likely that the new Queen Victoria exclaimed 'I will be good' – and that Queen Anne acknowledged that it was 'a fine day' – it is surely almost too good to be true that on hearing that his brother George III had died William IV announced he was going straight back to bed because he had 'never before slept with a queen'.

At the moment in question each of the individuals named above became in every sense the sovereign ruler of his or her realm, but of course not everyone who accedes to the thrown is eventually crowned. In April 1141, for example, Matilda, as the daughter of Henry I, was officially proclaimed 'Lady of the English' but she was never crowned. From April to June 1483 Edward V reigned, but on 25 June he was deposed before any coronation had taken place. The coronation of

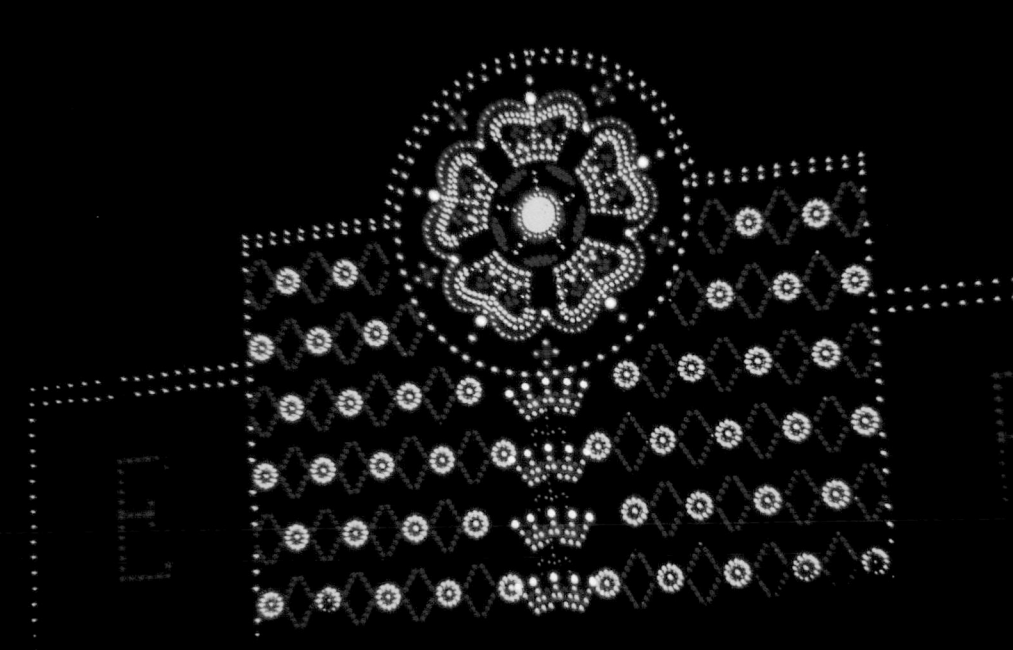

With rationing still in force, London needed an excuse to celebrate.

Night and day the celebrations continued.

Jane Seymour, Henry VIII's third wife, was postponed because of the plague only for her to die in childbirth before the ceremony could take place. (Arrangements were never even mooted for his fourth, fifth and sixth wives.)

Occasionally religious affiliations have got in the way of proceedings too, so that both Henrietta Maria of France and Catherine of Braganza went uncrowned because of the political difficulties arising from a habit the Stuart kings had of selecting wives from prominent Catholic families. Queen Anne's husband, George of Denmark, similarly missed out, largely it seems because no-one took him at all seriously. Charles II famously observed 'I have tried him drunk, and I have tried him sober and there is nothing in him' while Queen Victoria's dearest wish for her beloved Albert was that he would work to avoid the 'subordinate part played by the very stupid and insignificant husband of Queen Anne'. (This he certainly managed to do, but denied the title of king by the government of the day he had to content himself with the title of Prince Consort.) In fact Victoria's judgment now looks overly harsh, and Churchill's assessment of his character is probably closer to the mark: a staid and trustworthy man, he called him, 'without envy or ambition' and who loved his wife.

The same sadly cannot be said of George IV, who had Caroline of Brunswick physically barred from his coronation. On the day a phalanx of prize fighters was engaged to serve as pages, a prescient move as it turned out for the enraged queen spent the earlier part of the proceedings battering at the doors in an attempt to force her way into

the abbey, and the remainder wailing loudly when she was unable to do so. (In truth their marriage had got off to the shakiest of starts. For one thing George may well have been married already, illegally to his mistress Maria Fitzherbert; but he was also so shocked at the physical appearance of the woman he was expected to marry that, on meeting her for the first time, he demanded a servant bring him a large brandy. Caroline later complained that, horribly drunk on their wedding night, he made her smoke a pipe in bed, and later that she had stuck pins into a wax effigy of him before throwing it into the fire.)

For all that, however, by far the most significant individual to reign without a coronation must surely be Edward VIII. Not merely because this occurred within living memory – the announcement of his abdication was made in December 1936, the coronation having been planned for the following May – but because it was his decision to abandon this country in the way that he did that led directly to the events of 1953 and the sixtieth anniversary celebrations which are to take place this year.

Because of their significance and symbolism, the planning for a coronation has never been less than meticulous, and the most surprising little details can be intriguing. Who knew, for example, that Westminster Abbey was the first public building ever to be vacuum-cleaned? Ahead of Edward VII's coronation in 1902, the building was cleaned using 'Puffing Billy', the creation of inventor Herbert Cecil Booth and which featured a small 5hp electric motor sucking air through a cloth filter.

For hundreds of years Westminster Hall was similarly the scene of an extraordinary little pageant when, by tradition, a knight called the King's Champion (or Queen's, as appropriate) would appears at the Coronation Banquet to challenge any would-be usurpers. Traditionally the knight chosen was the Lord of the Manor of Scrivelsby, and technically it still is although sadly no-one has performed this rather romantic – if potentially dangerous – duty since 1821. Then the occasion was the last Coronation Banquet at Westminster Hall, which marked the coronation of George IV.

Nearly 800 years previously the aforementioned Lincolnshire manor had been granted by the Conqueror to one of his knights, a man called Marmion. The grant was 'by Grand Sergeanty, to wit, by the service of finding on the day of coronation, an armed knight who shall prove by his body, if need be, that the King is [the] true and rightful heir to the kingdom'. The present holder of the post, Lieutenant Colonel John Lindley Marmion Dymoke, is in theory liable for the same duty,

Vast stage sets were unlike anything seen before.

although in recent years the Champion has been called on to do nothing more onerous than to carry the Union Flag (or where appropriate the Banner for England) on certain state occasions.

Traditionally, in return for risking his life in his king's service, the Lord of the Manor was granted a number of handsome privileges besides the manor itself. These included the choice of the second best horse from the royal mews, together with saddle and armour and so forth; also the gold cup and cover from which the sovereign would drink his, the

Champion's, health. That said, much of it was provided only on a sort of sale-or-return basis, as the knight could collect the goods only in the event that his challenge was answered; but it is hard to conceive of a king allowing his own champion to go wanting.

In fact the King's (or Queen's) Champion was by no means the only courtier for whom a coronation offered the promise of a reward. For example an individual called the Lord Great Chamberlain is still responsible for handling all the 'domestic arrangements' when a sovereign enters the Palace of Westminster and for greeting her carriage as it arrives. Another hereditary post, it is unusual in that it is shared on a rotational basis between three aristocratic families who take over each time a new sovereign accedes to the throne. The Earl of Ancaster served George VI, and the Marquess of Cholmondeley has it for the duration of Elizabeth II's reign. At the conclusion of this it will pass to the 6th Lord Carrington or his heirs.

Like many ancient posts, such responsibilities are today purely ceremonial, and again because of its great antiquity holders can lay claim to some quite bizarre perquisites. Historically the new sovereign would have spent the night before the coronation sleeping at the palace, when the Lord Great Chamberlain would have been responsible for furnishing the royal bedchamber with linen and night garments and helping the incumbent to dress the following morning. In return for performing this once humble but increasingly prestigious service the holder of the post was permitted to request payment in kind. In practice this meant claiming the return of all the aforesaid garments together with the bed and bedding and any furniture in the room – and after the coronation itself the return of anything the new monarch was wearing, excepting for obvious reasons the state regalia.

The value of such a collection was potentially immense, and it was not unknown for the new sovereign to wriggle a little in an attempt to minimise his or her costs or indeed avoid handing over anything at all. The practice was not just longstanding, however, but enshrined in law thereby giving successive Lords Great Chamberlain something of the upper hand in any negotiations. Because of this James I, for example, was forced to hand over £200 in order to hang on to what he saw as his own possessions – a figure which could equate to as much as half a million pounds today if one compares earnings then with now – while Queen Anne is thought to have paid more than £300 just to keep the details of her bottom drawer to herself. Needless to say while the right may still exist it has not been claimed for quite a while, and certainly wasn't following the abbey's thirty-ninth coronation service in June 1953.

Even so, with their arcane perquisites and fancy dress, the Lord Great Chamberlain and the Queen's Champion are far from alone among the many office holders who for centuries have clustered around the Crown on these important state occasions. A number of other rural manors have traditionally come under the rules of Grand Sergeanty – meaning the Lord of the Manor is required to provide a service in place of payment – including those of Nether Bilsington in Kent and Sculton in Norfolk. Here the respective services include providing three bowls of maple wood for the Coronation Banquet, and serving as Larderer for the occasion.

Perhaps the most celebrated of the manors, however, is that of Kenninghall in Norfolk where since Norman times the required service has been to fill the post of *Pincera Regis* or Chief Butler (with the Lord Mayor of London serving as assistant) and Chief Carver. Once again the post technically still exists but although no-one has performed such a service since the nineteenth century, this has not prevented individuals with a vested interest from seeking to ensure that their ancient rights are recognised and protected in law. The reality is that while, to modern ears, butlering may sound like a subservient role, proximity to the sovereign has always been sought and even in relatively recent times it can be jealously guarded.

In 1902, for example, full consideration was given to holding a Coronation Banquet for Edward VII, in which case the Chief Butler might well have been summoned. Unfortunately His Majesty's ill-health meant plans were put on hold and not revisited, but this may have been no bad thing for ahead of the coronation a row was already brewing with no fewer than three powerful individuals claiming the right to serve as *Pincera Regis*. The three were His Grace the 16th Duke of Norfolk, a descendant of William de Albini who had been granted the Manor of Kenninghall by Henry I, and a Mr Taylor who by this time owned the manor. Fortunately the postponement of the banquet meant no decision had to be made as to which of the three had the strongest claim – and nor has it since, which may be no bad thing.

Interestingly the first of them, the duke, already had a highly significant role to play (as indeed his descendant still does today) as the Earl Marshal and Hereditary Marshal of England. Another Norman creation – descending from William the Marshal, who arrived in England with the Conqueror in 1066 – the holder of this hereditary post performs a number of important duties for the Crown. These include having overall responsibility for the State Opening of Parliament each year, also for all state funerals, for the conduct of the College of Arms (the controlling body for all heraldic and genealogical disputes and judgements) – and of course for coronations.

Looking back along the Mall.

The Mall through Admirals Arch.

Grandstands provided the best possible view.

… but obscured landmarks for the photographers!

The temporary pavilion at the abbey.

Banners beneath 'Big Ben'.

Scaffolding fails to spoil and iconic view.

3

WENT THE DAY BADLY

Unfortunately, as an hereditary appointment, the heavy responsibilities of the Earl Marshal's role can occasionally fall on the wrong shoulders and more than once they have done so.

The 5th Duke of Norfolk, for example, was a lunatic and having been effectively exiled to Italy, the duties of Earl Marshal were hastily devolved to his brother. By all accounts he did a good job, and the fact that the Fitzalan-Howards still retain the post after more than 500 years – during which time members of the family have been persecuted for being Catholic, attainted and even beheaded – suggests that on the whole they have understood perfectly the demands of the role. Even in the right hands, however, when everything is well organised, perfectly planned and minutely regulated, things can still go wrong at coronations – and not infrequently they have.

At the coronation of Henry IV in 1399, for example, His Majesty lost a shoe, then a spur and finally the wind blew the crown from his head. In such superstitious times all three events were certain to be taken as ill-omens, and when a fortune teller prophesied that the king would meet his death in Jerusalem his advisers doubtless counselled him against travelling to the Holy Land. In fact he never did, but he was doomed nevertheless, and fourteen years later, after being taken ill while at prayer in Westminster Abbey, he was carried into the abbot's lodgings and made comfortable. Unfortunately the room he was placed in was one the monks called the Jerusalem Chamber – it's still there today – and on hearing this Henry was minded to recall the prophecy, and died shortly afterwards.

Henry perhaps can hardly be blamed, but it has to be said that more than once the sovereign has scarcely helped to ensure that things run smoothly. Since as long ago as 1308, for instance, all anointed sovereigns of England (until 1603, and after that date of Great Britain) have chosen to be seated at the moment of their coronation. Traditionally they have used St Edward's Chair which was commissioned in 1296 (by Edward I although it is named after Edward the Confessor) and designed to hold the sacred Stone of Scone. From the earliest times both chair and stone were kept in the abbey's shrine of St Edward's Chapel, although since 1996 there has been an agreement for the latter to reside in Scotland except when it is required for ceremonial usage. The chair itself is a high-backed gothic design carved in oak by Master Carpenter Walter, who reportedly received 100s for his work, a very considerable sum in thirteenth-century England. Once highly painted and gilded the chair today looks just old and exceedingly plain, with much of the decoration lost to graffiti and initials carved by pilgrims and Victorian choirboys. It was also sadly bomb-damaged in 1914 – by suffragettes rather than Germany – so now lives in a more secure position by the tomb of Henry V.

Long one of the abbey's most important treasures, it was nevertheless deemed unsuitable by Mary I who refused even to touch it on the grounds that it had been polluted by the Protestant devil Edward V. Queen Anne had a problem with it too, in that she was simply too large to fit in it. Mary was the first queen to be crowned at Westminster in her own right (Elizabeth II is the sixth) although one would have thought that as a famously testy Catholic her intransigence might have been foreseen.

Decorations on the Strand.

Tiers of seating brought London to life.

The weather was dull, but the mood and the colours stayed bright.

Similarly Anne's obesity was impossible to conceal so it seems extraordinary that no-one saw there might be a problem there as well. One wonders, too, how it was that Charles II's coronation was planned and then postponed – had really nobody noticed that Cromwell had disposed of all the symbolic regalia? – and how could the Archbishop of Canterbury manage to have jammed the Coronation Ring onto the wrong finger of Queen Victoria, particularly when the abbey authorities had gone to the trouble of having a new one made to fit her famously tiny hand?

He was nervous, perhaps, and who can blame him given the gravity of such a great state occasion, and the heavy responsibility of placing on his sovereign's finger what has long been considered 'the wedding ring of England'. Apparently that was the reason given for several of the upsets at George VI's coronation, when for example the Lord Great Chamberlain failed to affix the Sword of State properly (the king had to do it himself) and then, as one of the priests fell in a faint onto the floor, the Crown was put onto the king's head back to front.

Perhaps one should not be surprised then that, if the officials cannot always be trusted to do these things properly, the congregation certainly cannot. In 1308 the guests almost rioted at the coronation of Edward II, in protest at the quality of the food and the tactless decision of the king's favourite Piers Gaveston to array himself in purple. Similarly in 1761, after complaints that George III's coronation had gone on for too long, many of the guests sat down to eat, drowning out much of the remaining ceremony with the clattering of their cutlery.

Today this sounds a little crass perhaps, but clearing up after our own queen's coronation the Westminster Abbey cleaners found not

Crowds throng the Mall.

Buckingham Palace became the focus of the world.

The decorations were both colourful and imaginative.

just the inevitable items of lost property – including three ropes of pearls, more than a dozen brooches, six bracelets, several diamonds and twenty golden balls which had presumably dropped off peers' coronets – but also countless sandwich wrappers together with orange peel and apple cores, and an undisclosed but substantial quantity of empty liqueur bottles. (The BBC's Richard Dimbleby expressed special horror at this last thing, complaining about how remarkable it

was 'that even on this occasion we could not break ourselves of one of our worst national habits.') But far worse was the discovery that a royal cypher had been hacked from one of the chairs, apparently by a souvenir hunter with a ticket for what one might term one of the expensive seats. Not everyone was entirely surprised, however, for as the long-suffering Earl Marshal was later to observe of his fellow peers, 'They're capable of anything.'

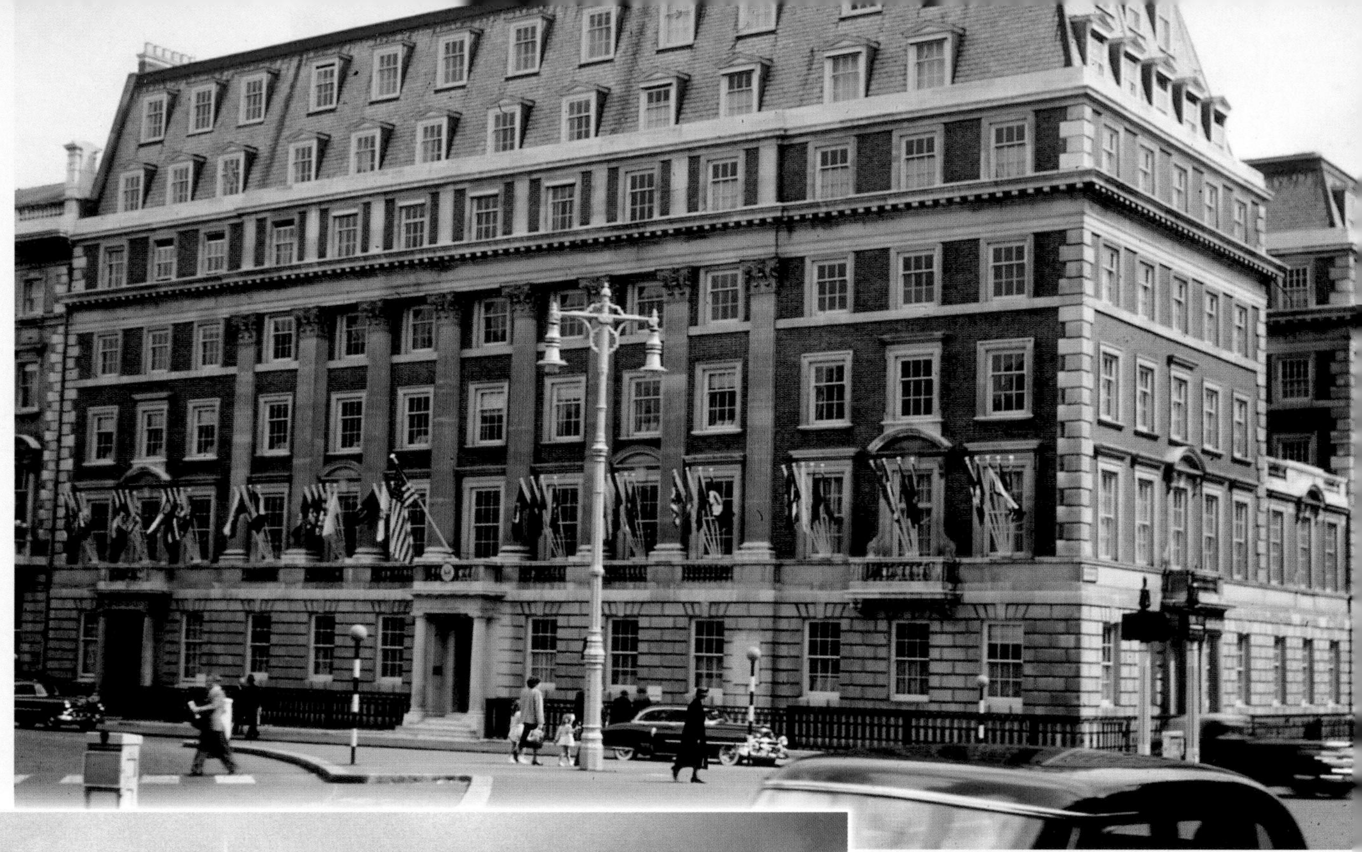

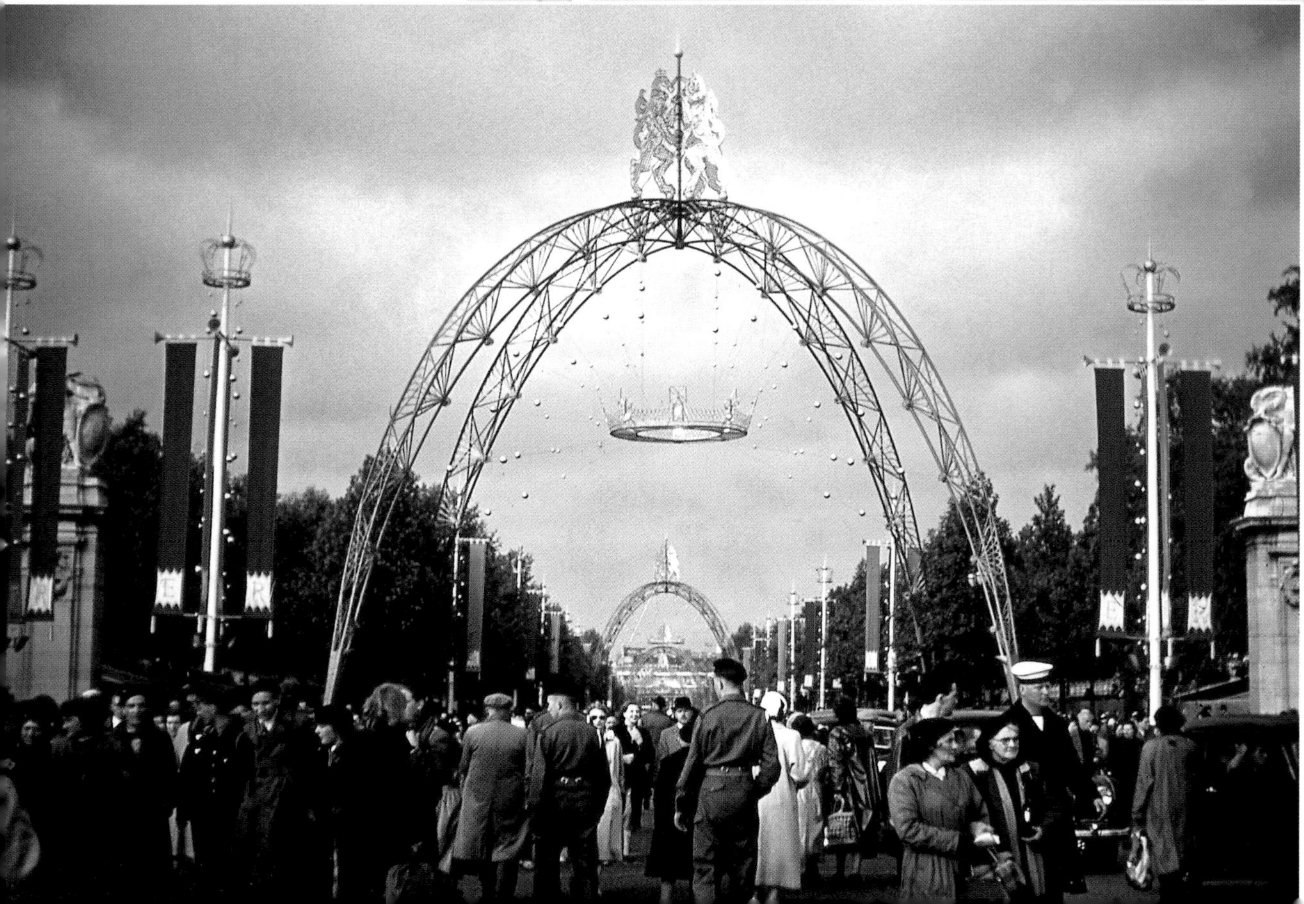
E
R

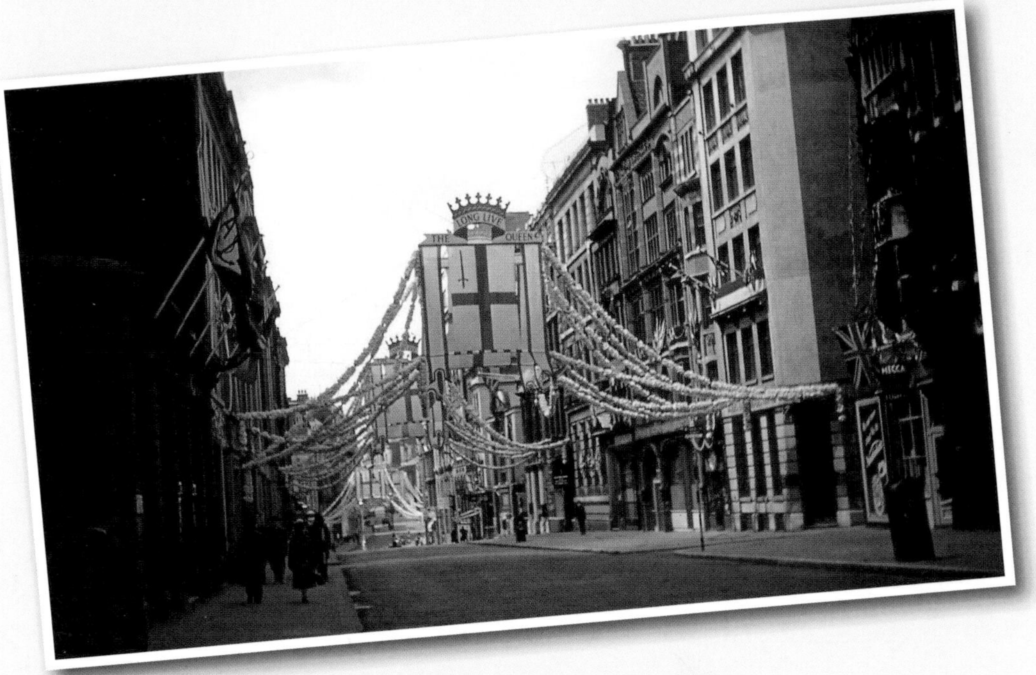
LONG LIVE
THE
QUEEN
MECCA

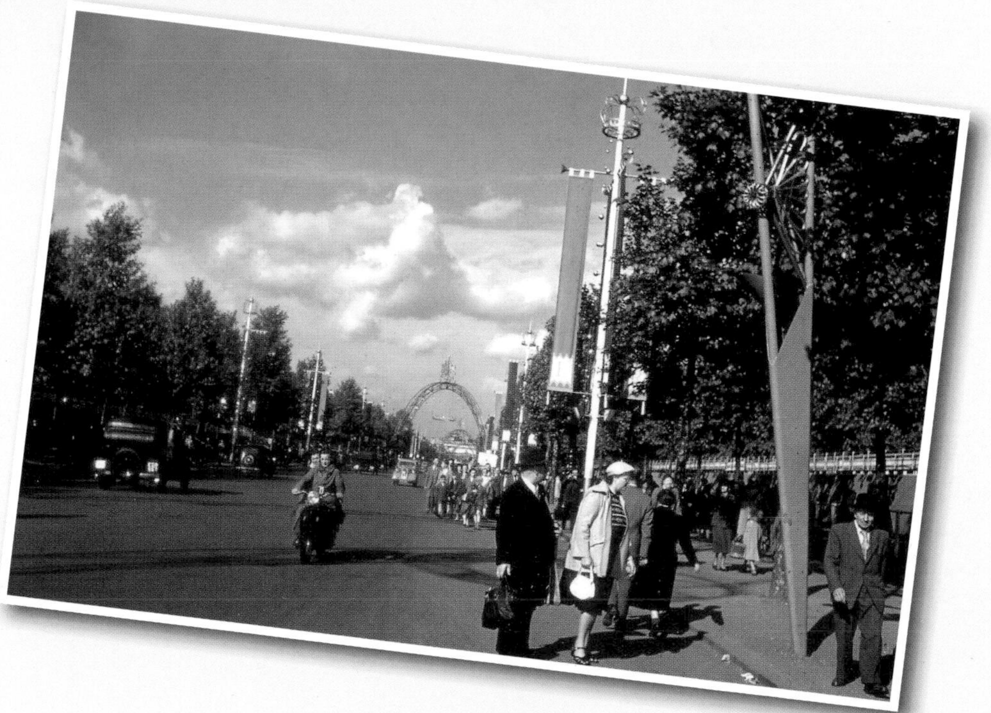

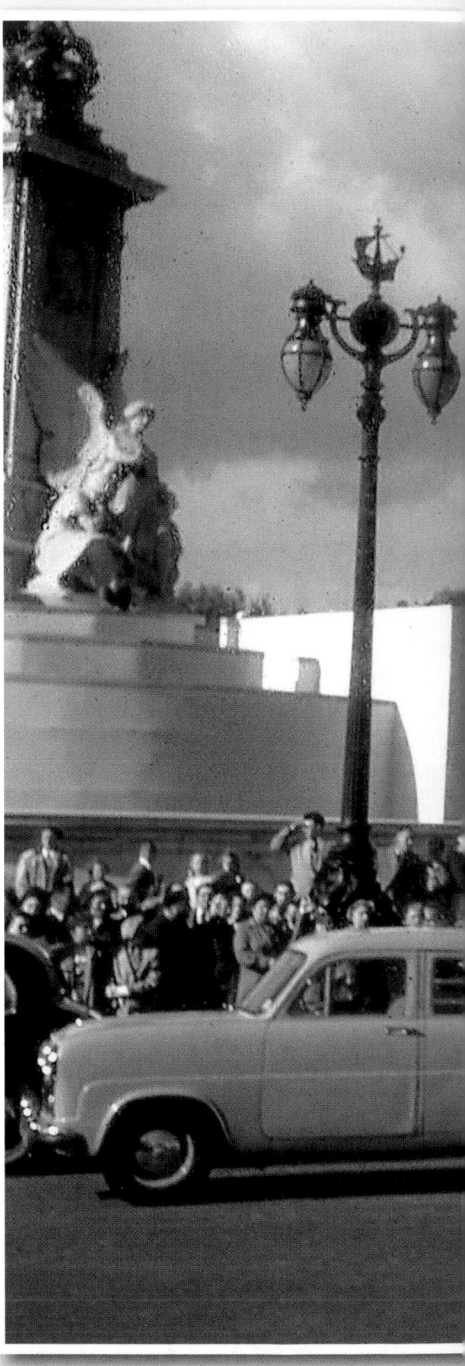

Unfamiliar structures began to spring up …

4

PREPARATIONS BEGIN

The date for the coronation was agreed very soon after the death of George VI, the decision taken for nearly sixteen months to pass in order to allow for a period of personal and official mourning and of course for the complex preparations for the event itself.

As early as New Year's Day 1953, Westminster Abbey closed to the public and extensive work began on its transformation into what was in effect to be a stage for the world. A full-time workforce at least 200-strong was engaged, charged with the construction of huge ranks of tiered, theatre seating (to accommodate an astonishing 8,251 guests) together with new staircases and flooring. Outside a substantial but temporary annex was constructed at the abbey's western end, a covered area in which guests could gather and organise themselves either side of the processions to and from church.

Before the annex were also to be placed immense representations of the Queen's Beasts, ten large-scale sculptures commissioned by the Ministry of Works from the sculptor James Woodford. When completed each of the plaster figures was some 6ft in height, the impressive display including the most familiar icons – the Lion of England, the Unicorn of Scotland and the Welsh Red Dragon of Cadwallader – as well as a number of somewhat more unusual, even recondite heraldic creatures. In no particular order these were the Falcon of the Plantagenets, the Black Bull of Clarence, the White Lion of Mortimer, the Griffin of Edward III, the White Greyhound of Richmond, the White Horse of Hanover and the Yale of Beaufort, a kind of swivel-horned goat or antelope, from the Hebrew word *yael*.

Happily all ten still exist, and after a period on display at Hampton Court Palace and then Windsor Castle the collection crossed the Atlantic to be placed in the care of the Canadian Museum of Civilization in Gatineau. (Perhaps even more fortunately a set of replicas was created in the late-1950s in Portland stone, at the expense of an Edinburgh drinks magnate. These can be seen on display at the Royal Botanic Gardens in Kew, and more details on the beasts themselves can be found in a short appendix to this book.)

… and heraldic symbols were everywhere.

For obvious reasons, in 1953 the focus was always going to be on London and the ancient City of Westminster, although many other parts of the United Kingdom were invited to send representatives as well to assist in the preparation of the abbey precinct for the ceremony and indeed in dressing the new queen and her attendants.

Up in Scotland, for example, immense quantities of blue and gold carpeting were being woven for the abbey floor and the new seating areas. In all, more than 2,964 square yards were produced on what at the time was said to be the widest carpet loom in the world, a 33ft monster operated by Messrs James Templeton & Co. of Kerr Street, Glasgow. This, incidentally, was the self-same workshop which had produced the heraldic designs used to carpet the abbey in 1911 for the coronation of the queen's grandfather George V.

Further south in Bradford some 4,000 yards of velvet were produced to cover 2,000 chairs and an incredible 5,700 stools, and at the old market town of Braintree in Essex millworkers employed by Warner & Sons spent more than ten weeks under the direction of Alec Hunter hand-weaving 20 yards of luxurious crimson velvet for Her Majesty's robe. By this time hand-weaving of this sort was already a rare process, but with a tradition of supplying the royal household dating back to Victoria's reign, Warner & Sons was clearly highly experienced and the obvious choice.

Because of its expertise with silk and velvet the company was also commissioned to weave a new blue silk and gold lurex thread fabric called Queensway, which had been designed by Robert Godden who was at this time Rector of the Royal College of Art in London. Depicting for the first time on such an occasion the heraldic emblems of all four constituent parts of the United Kingdom – meaning the rose, thistle, shamrock and leek of England, Scotland, Ireland and the Principality of Wales respectively – it was produced in great quantities. As much as 1,500 yards were transported to London and used to create hangings for the balconies in the abbey and at the front of the royal box. Happily much of the original cloth still survives, and as recently as 2010 a fragment from the company's archive joined no fewer than ten other items from the county which were selected by the British Museum for the landmark BBC series *A History of the World in 100 Objects*.

As a gift from the queen to mark her coronation five new blue and gold silk copes were also created by skilled craftsmen for the Dean and Chapter of Westminster. These incorporated representations of the two senior and most traditional heraldic beasts – the lion and unicorn – although in the event only four were worn on the day. (The Dean preferred a much older cope which had been made for the coronation of Charles II.) At the same time Edgington's flag factory at Sidcup in Kent was busy preparing special flags, complete with hand-painted cartouches.

By 20 May the construction works in the abbey were largely finished, and daily rehearsals began, occasionally with members of the royal family in attendance although only rarely the new sovereign herself. Ahead of the many others, individuals involved in the ceremony had also been working to perfect their own contribution, for example the sixty-strong orchestra and 400-strong choir which would be supplementing the efforts of the abbey's resident choristers. Not entirely surprisingly the size of the chorus was to cause its own problems, and from the start two assistants were on hand to relay instructions from the Conductor and Director of Music to those located too far away from him to see the movements of his baton or in positions which were obscured by portions of the abbey structure.

The form of the coronation service itself was fortunately already well understood by those most closely involved, so needed little attention. Known to descend directly from the service used at the crowning of King Edgar, in Bath in 973, it could genuinely be said to be well-tried and tested. Since the coronation of Elizabeth I the original fourteenth-century order of service was no longer written in Latin, but otherwise very few modifications had been made over time. Thus the queen, for example, was required to speak a mere thirty-four words during the course of a two-and-a-half hour service, but nevertheless Her Majesty reportedly spent a considerable amount of time rehearsing her lines. (As much as any actress would, said the press, reporters both here and abroad eagerly but respectfully documenting every tiny detail they could lay hands on.)

Also involved in many hundreds of hours of preparation and rehearsal, of course, were the thousands of well-drilled servicemen and women who traditionally make such a glorious spectacle of this country's great national occasions. Come June the processions to and from the abbey were to be more than 16,000-strong, and it has since been estimated that well over 29,000 uniformed individuals would have been on the streets of central London on the day itself. These would have included in excess of 2,500 servicemen from around the Commonwealth, between them providing a dazzling and wildly diverse display every bit as multicultural in tone and appearance as anything London could show visitors today[*].

For Londoners and others the rehearsals proved almost as great a draw as the actual coronation parades, despite starting in the early hours. Tens of thousands of people packed into the Mall to see the dummy runs, as numerous carriages and the Coach of State (empty, its blinds drawn down) made their way along the processional route. Inevitably the media was there too, and in force, with Pathé News producing a short reel for cinema-goers about the rehearsals. The latter also boasted about how many cameramen the company would have on the day – more than thirty, for at least one of whom this was to be his fourth coronation – and highlighting its reliance on the latest technology. This included what was widely referred to as 'the largest telephoto lens in the world' and a very special zoom lens which was said to have cost £1,000, or about the same as three Morris Minor motor cars.

From early April, regular rehearsals had been taking place in the air as well. Under the watchful command of Air Vice-Marshal the Earl of Bandon, scores of pilots and ground crew from the Royal Air Force

---

[*]   An approximate breakdown indicates there were 3,600 members of the Royal Navy present, 16,100 from the Army and 7,000 from the RAF as well as 2,000 from Commonwealth forces and 500 from the colonies. Some 6,700 reserve and administrative troops were also present with 1,000 officers and men of the Royal Military Police brought in to supplement the men of the Metropolitan force. A further 7,000 police were drawn from seventy-five provincial forces, with those on foot marching ten abreast while servicemen on horseback were six abreast.

Familiar buildings disappeared beneath the decorations …

… as London prepared for the party.

Fighter Command and the Royal Canadian Air Force had spent weeks preparing 144 Gloster Meteors and two dozen Canadair F-86 Sabres for a special Coronation Day air display.

Lord Bandon's plan was for a massed flypast over Buckingham Palace at just 1,200ft, and basing his men at Biggin Hill in Kent from the beginning of May he set in place a rigorous training programme. The 168 jets were to form up over the Thames estuary. To assist the lead pilots, who would have been flying fighters with only the most rudimentary onboard navigational aids, illuminated beacons would be placed on several of central London's tallest office blocks. Using these as a guide, the aircraft were to fly in tight formation up the river and along the Mall before passing over the balcony of Buckingham Palace at thirty-second intervals from where the royal family would take the salute.

Back on the ground, and to be found among the varied uniforms of the many different service bodies involved, were huge numbers of police. Not just the Metropolitan force were called in, but also men of the Royal Military Police, the Royal Canadian Mounted Police, and from the various county forces who were charged with bussing teams in from around the country. Surrey, for example, sent eighty-three men, mostly to help line the processional route along the Mall rather than to head off any specified criminal or public-order threat.

Assembled in London the combined constabularies' final rehearsal was arranged for the day before the coronation itself, individual policemen being positioned at intervals along the route and standing to attention between guardsmen from the Grenadiers and Coldstream. Already informed of their positions, their day was to start with a briefing and inspection by the Home Secretary at 10 a.m. with ranks of tents pitched in Green Park where the men would return to spend a largely sleepless night ahead of a 3 a.m. reveille on the big day.

Of course the success of any great day of pageantry and display depends on rehearsals of this sort, as well as on meticulous planning and painstaking attention to detail by those involved in the organisation. By far the most important rehearsals, however – and easily the most secret – were the two full dress rehearsals involving the young queen and other members of the royal family. These were held at the abbey on 22 May and then again exactly a week later, using replicas of the Crown Jewels although in all other regards they followed faithfully the programme for the actual coronation day.

At other times many somewhat smaller gatherings took place at the abbey, often with Her Grace the Duchess of Norfolk taking the queen's position (as wife of the first Peer of the Kingdom). These were held to ensure that everyone else taking part in the procession through the nave of Westminster Abbey understood fully his or her role, and was completely familiar with the order of service and the requirements this placed on them[*]. Guests were expected to partake as well, where possible, the society diarist James Lees-Milne observing the duchess at one of them and noting how 'the weight of the Orb and Sceptre in either hand called for much balancing about physical strength'.

Nothing could be done about anyone's nerves, perhaps, but practice clearly makes perfect. Now more than at any time in literally 1,000 years it was essential that everyone understood this and grasped the great symbolism of the day and the need for absolute precision in the tiniest gesture and inflection. After all, come June, it wasn't just the 8,251 guests in Westminster Abbey who would be witnesses to the coronation, but – for the first time in history – literally millions of people in London, across the country, and around the world.

---

[*] The Sovereign's procession, as it entered the abbey, numbered some 250 representatives of the Crown, Church and State. It included Church leaders, Commonwealth prime ministers, members of the Royal Household, civil and military leaders, and in their splendid livery the Yeoman of the Guard.

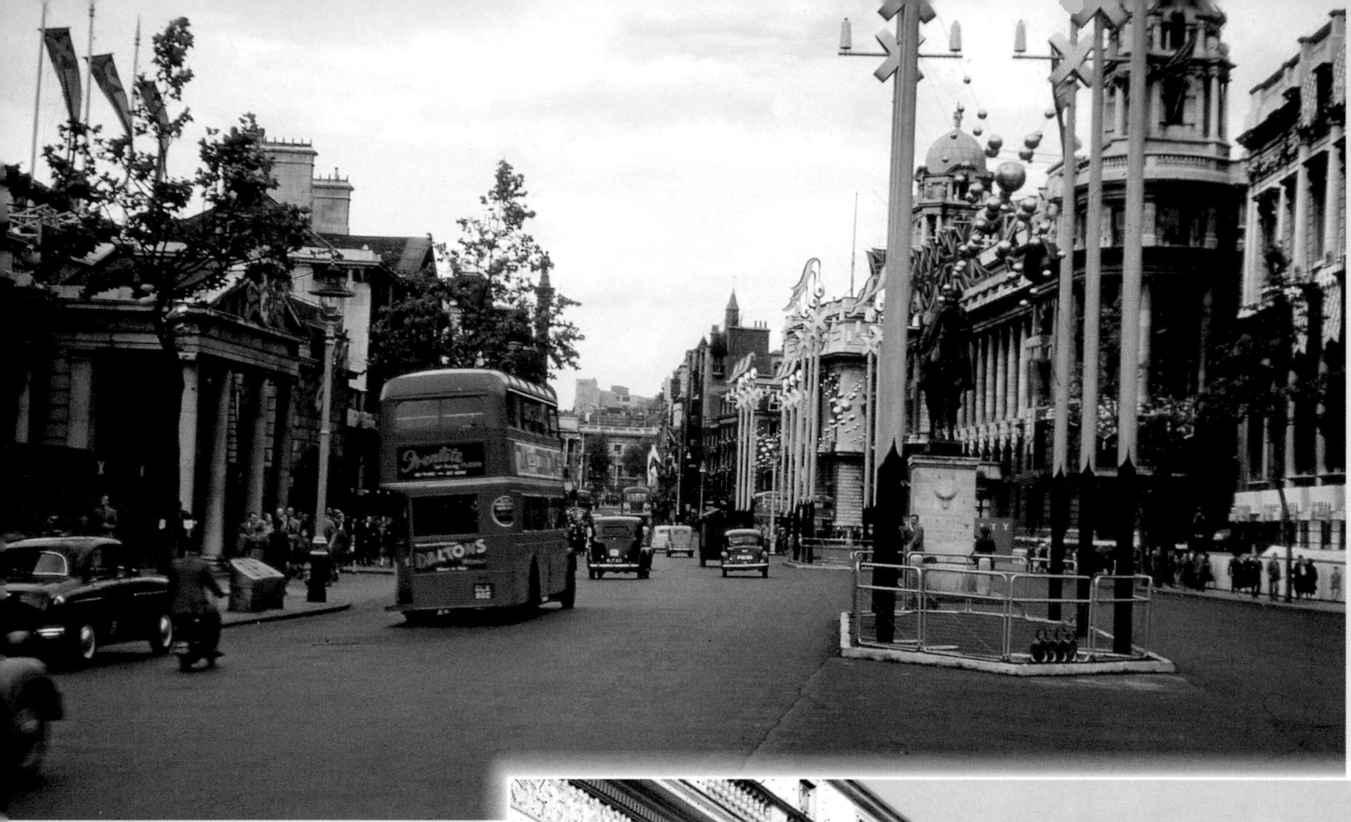
DALTONS

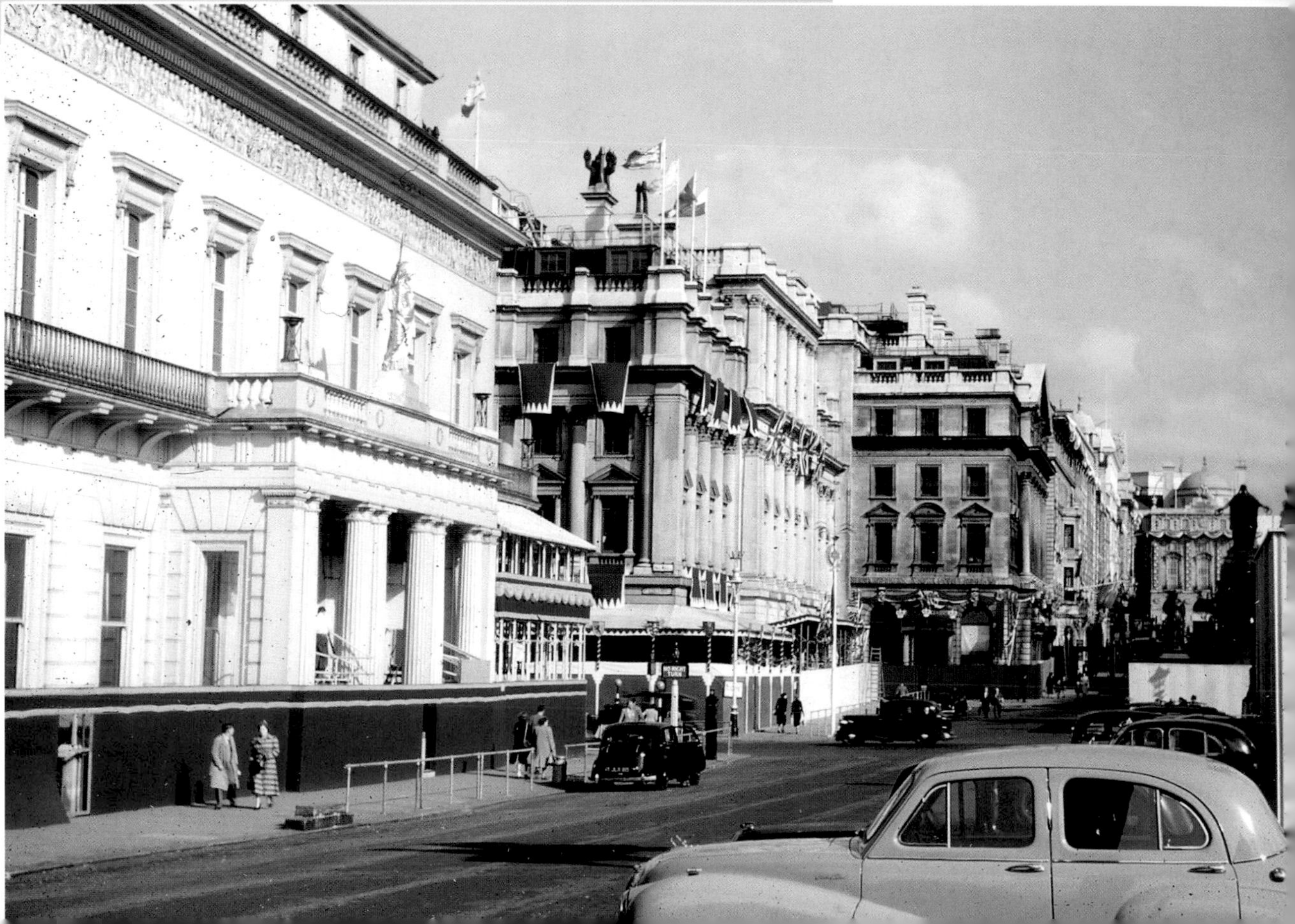

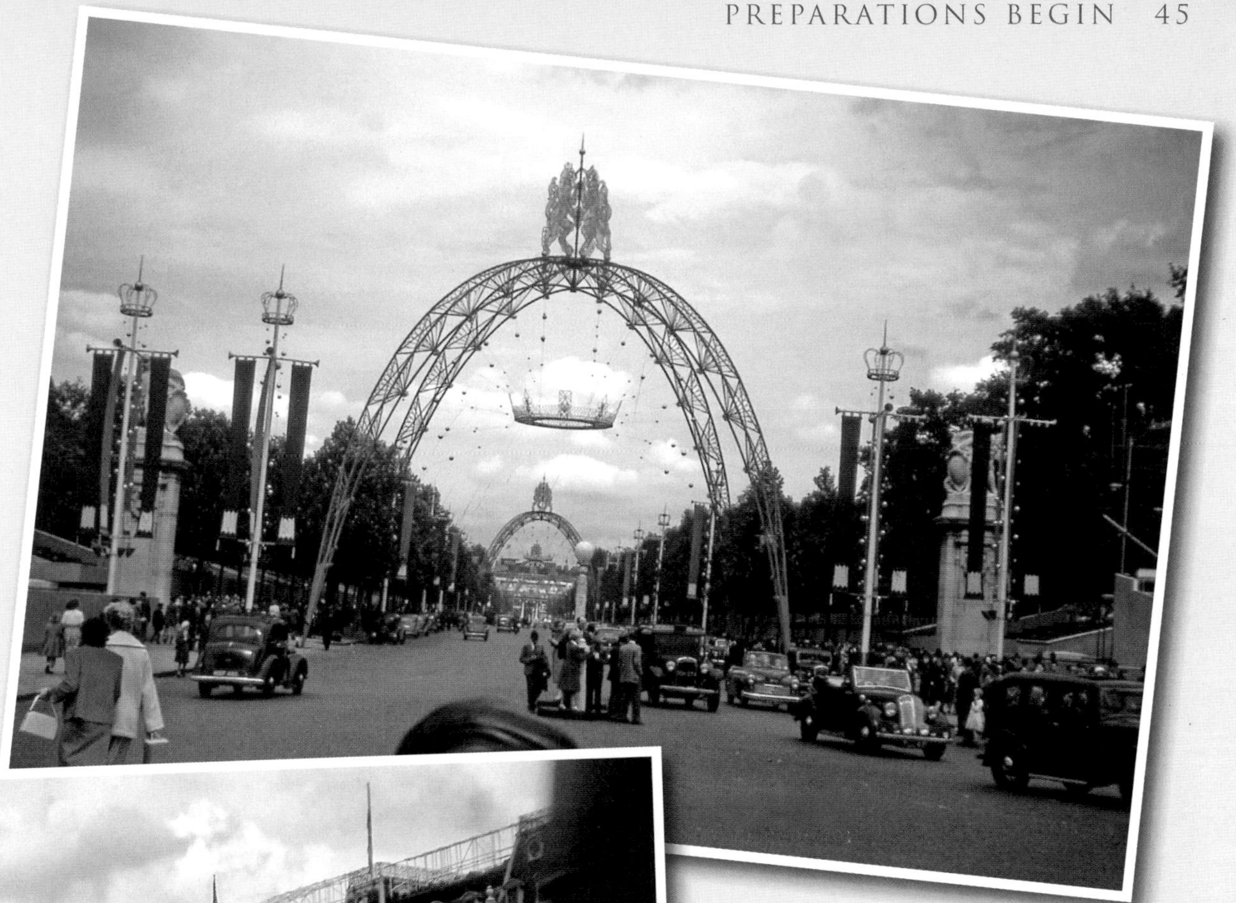

VOTRIX
WRIGLEYS
RAINCOATS
Ever-Ready
Criterion
Restaurant
PLEASURE GARDENS
BATTERSEA PARK
KEEP LEFT

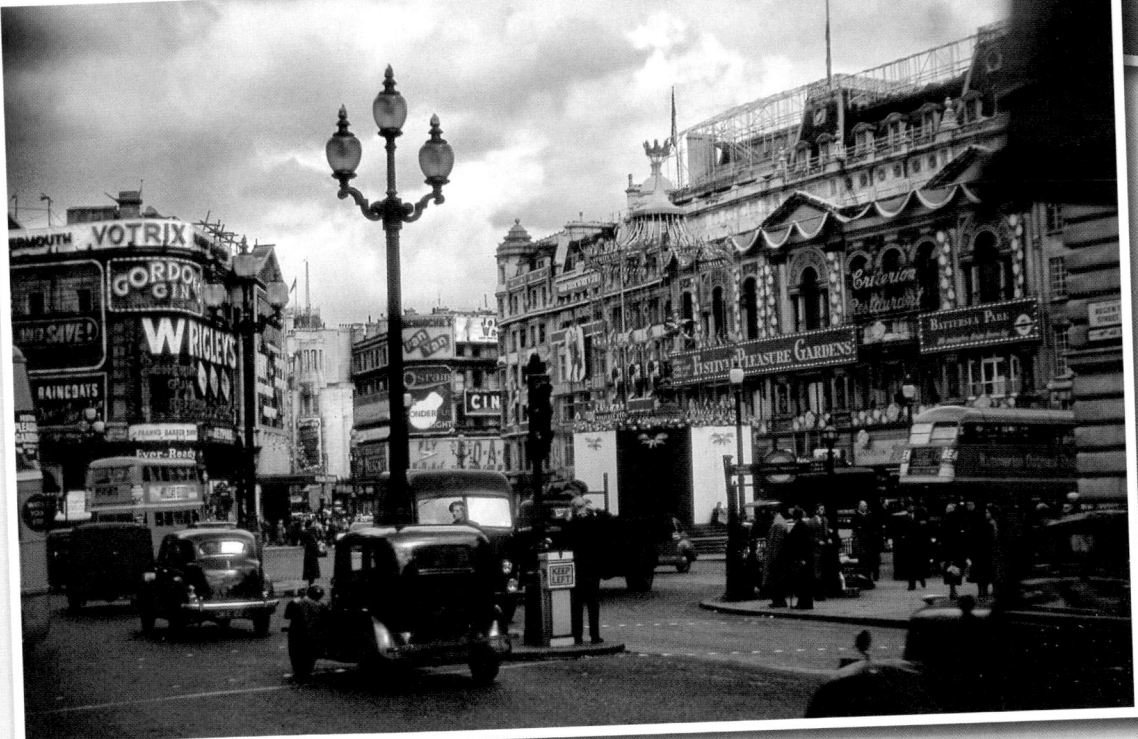

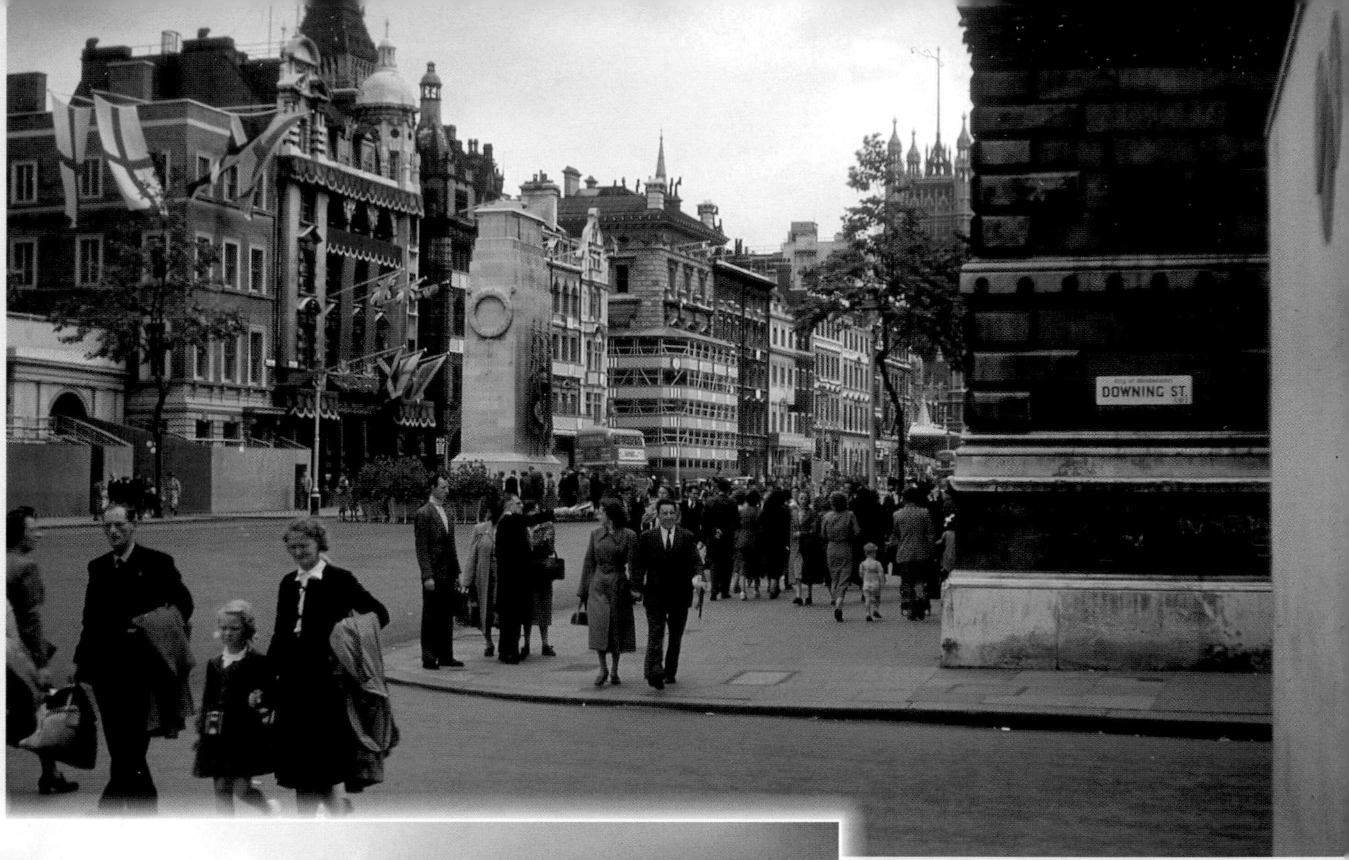
DOWNING ST.

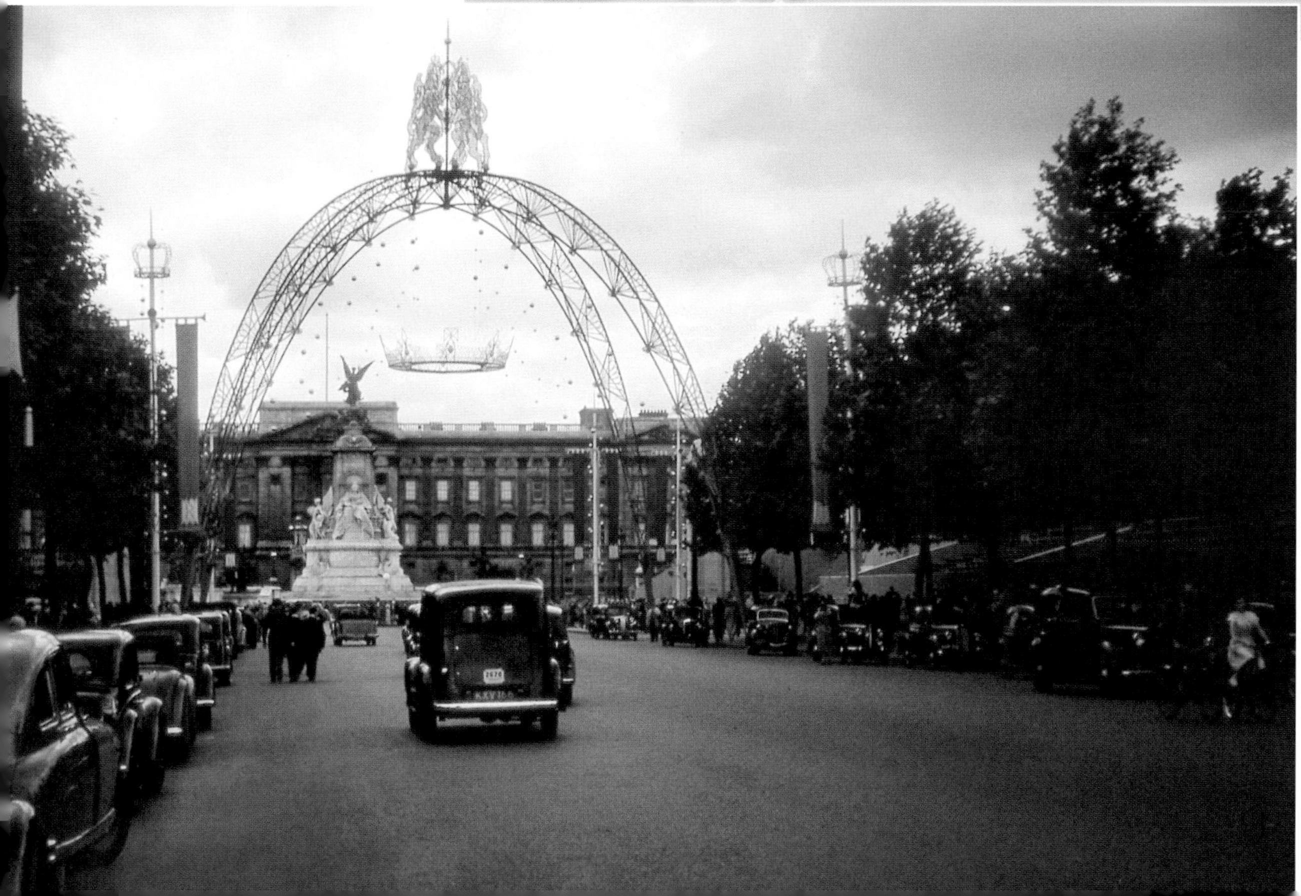

Whitehall readies itself …

… whilst a hero looks on.

5

LIGHTS, CAMERAS ... ACTION

The numbers of viewers and listeners are naturally dwarfed by the standards of our own globalised twenty-four-hour multimedia world, but sixty years ago the coronation of Elizabeth II was quite literally an event without parallel. The very first great BBC television spectacular to be seen by a mass audience, more than twenty-seven million viewers spent the day perched on the edge of their seats in order to make the most of the flickering black-and-white images passing across the kind of tiny 9in or 14in screens which typified the average home television set[*].

The queen herself was said to be undaunted by the prospect of such a huge audience, to such a degree indeed that when a courtier asked if she felt nervous Her Majesty replied that 'Aureole will be fine' in the mistaken belief that the enquiry was a reference to a favourite colt of hers which was running in the Derby the following week. In the event the queen's horse came in only second, but the anecdote speaks volumes about the twenty-five-year-old's self-confidence and her apparently unshakeable belief in her own destiny.

For all that, however, the decision to allow the cameras into the abbey – in the Victorian Walter Bagehot's oft-repeated phrase to 'let in daylight upon magic' – was by no means a straightforward one. Away from the public's gaze, discussions as to whether to do it or not had been lively and protracted, something which seems extraordinary in this day and age when there is never any question that the public should be invited – even encouraged – to enjoy the pomp and ceremony of these great state occasions.

In 1937, as part of King George VI's coronation celebrations, and for its first ever outside broadcast, the BBC had been permitted to film along the route of the coronation procession. Edited highlights from this were broadcast later rather than live, and in all likelihood they were seen by no more than 10,000 people at home as the Corporation's new high-definition television service had commenced only the previous November and was at this time still prohibitively expensive. By 1953 things had improved somewhat although at a time when a manual labourer might expect to earn around £10 a week, the buyer of a television set with a 14in screen would be unlikely to see any change from £60.

Between the queen's accession and her coronation there was nevertheless a major public debate about how, and indeed whether, the ceremony should be televised, much as there was years later over proposals to televise debates in the House of Commons and the House of Lords and – more recently still – the proceedings of the courts during major trials.

Traditionalists, unsurprisingly, opposed the proposals outright. Many were offended at the idea of filming within such an important religious building; others worried that opening the proceedings up to so many eyes (and using this new-fangled and profane technology) risked damaging or at least demystifying the almost magical working of authority and the monarchy. Some, including Prime Minister Churchill, also objected to the notion of turning the day into a mere entertainment.

---

[*] At a time when the total population of the United Kingdom was slightly in excess of thirty-six million, this figure includes viewers watching BBC feeds around the world.

The colourful sweep of Royal Street.

Interestingly there were also, even then, widespread concerns that if such a sacred ceremony were transformed into what we would term a mass media event, the result could be exploited by the government of the day or more likely by private companies. (In the USA the coverage was frequently interrupted by advertisements, something considered on this side of the Atlantic to be vulgar and lacking in respect and which just a year later was mentioned as a possible objection to the establishment in Britain of a rival to the BBC in the form of the commercial network ITV.)

On the other side of the argument were the populists (including, it was suspected, the new queen herself). They wished to democratise the proceedings and to see the coronation celebrated as an authentically national event rather than as just another exclusive, quasi-Masonic ritual intended to be observed by only a relatively small and decidedly Establishment elite.

Early attempts at bridging this divide included a suggestion that events only as far as the choir screen would be televised and broadcast live, with the remainder filmed and then released at a later date. Most obviously this would allow for any errors to be excised from the version the public saw. For the anti-lobby it was also felt that such an arrangement might return some prestige to the privileged classes, guests in the abbey who might otherwise be deprived of the exclusive opportunity to witness at first hand the crowning of the new monarch if they had in some way to share the experience with the great unwashed.

Unfortunately this would have prevented the television audience from witnessing the actual moment Her Majesty was crowned – or at least stopped them seeing it until some time later. Not unnaturally the public was less than impressed with the whole idea, as indeed was the press, and after some highly effective flame-fanning from the latter the matter was eventually debated in Parliament. Here, following some heated arguments, it was finally decided that the entire ceremony should be televised and broadcast live, with the sole exception of the anointing and communion, the same two portions of the service which had not even been photographed during previous coronations.

Subsequently, albeit not until the 1980s, it was revealed that the reversal followed the personal intervention of the queen. In what looks like an early example of her famously sure hand and her adroitness when it comes to juggling the desires and demands of a modern constitutional monarchy, Her Majesty is believed to have reminded the politicians that it was she who was being crowned not the Cabinet. For this reason she made it plain that she felt that all her subjects should have the opportunity of witnessing the event, and not just the usual favoured few.

While emphatically not the point, Her Majesty's steadfastness on this point and its result were very greatly to increase interest in television among the British public. As previously described, sales of new home sets leapt on the news that the ceremony would be televised and broadcast live, and it is now estimated that the proceedings in the abbey were watched by something over half of the adult population in this country compared to just under a third who listened to the service on the wireless.

Viewing figures were to be particularly high in London and the Midlands, where there were around three times as many television viewers as radio listeners. Admittedly more than half the viewers would see the ceremony in the homes of others, and approximately one and a half million on big-screen relays shown in cinemas and other public venues. To these can be added a very special group of just 200 children, patients at London's famous Great Ormond Street Hospital, who watched the show in colour with the moving images beamed to them on a closed circuit from three colour cameras overlooking Parliament Square.

All this, of course, was yet to happen, but looking back exactly sixty years later it can truly be said that Coronation Day 1953 was the very moment at which television in Britain became a genuinely mass medium for communication. No less significantly the huge interest in the BBC's programming that day was also to provide the clearest possible demonstration of how well the new queen understood her subjects, and how well she knew what they wanted.

Fortunately, and despite the lengthy and tiresome debates for and against cameras being admitted to the abbey in this way, the BBC still found itself with a full year to organise its coverage of this special

Parliament Square transformed.

Flags festoon Whitehall, the Cenotaph for once forgotten.

and unique event. The resources it chose to devote to the day were substantial, especially given the relatively small size of the sole national broadcaster at this time. The team they assembled included a dedicated group of 120 people, together with five cameras actually inside the abbey and others located outside at twenty-one strategic points along the processional route. On the site of the Colonial Office, with an estimated 2,000 journalists and 500 photographers from ninety-two nations in attendance, there was also an entirely new facility, a 90ft wooden hut able to handle thirty different broadcasts simultaneously.

Today the single person most associated with the television coverage is the seasoned broadcaster Richard Dimbleby who provided the running commentary to accompany the television pictures. (John Snagge provided a similar service to radio listeners.) As a result, few if any outside the industry recall the name of Peter Dimmock who, as the BBC's head of outside broadcasts, was largely responsible for the organisation of the now celebrated coverage. The challenges which faced him were many and various, but most obviously there was a need for the equipment to be silent and discreet and to be positioned where it would not impede or obstruct members of the clergy, the royal family and so forth.

The new theatre seating, the large orchestra and choir, and of course the more than 8,000 guests also placed a high premium on space so that Dimmock was required to go to great lengths to find space for his crews. So great, indeed, that a search began for 'small, inconspicuous' cameramen – not that cameramen as a breed were in these pioneering days exactly numerous. Because they were expected to work from within compact wooden enclosures, those chosen for the work also needed to be unusually supple.

One of them, senior cameraman Dennis Montague, an ex-RAF man who filmed the actual moment of the placing of the crown, afterwards said he had 'evolved various kneeling positions' in order to cope with the low roof of what the crew soon nicknamed 'the dog kennels'. In fact Montague was one of the lucky ones: a junior colleague called Anthony 'Bud' Flanagan was partly buried beneath the floor, secreting himself into a tiny compartment underneath his camera. Positioned among the musicians of the orchestra, Flanagan discovered that the spike from one of the cellos came between his feet, and that the cellist had occasionally to pass his bow beneath the camera once the music started.

Further restrictions were placed on the men by the timetabling of the event, and its numerous rehearsals, so that as mere technicians they were ordered not to leave their positions without permission, or indeed to

Parliament Square, with the abbey behind.

answer the call of nature without a member of the abbey staff personally escorting them from their station.

Some indication of how seriously all this was taken can be gauged from the example of another cameraman who, after being ticked off by Dimmock because his white shirt was visible from somewhere in the congregation, was ordered to buy a new one, as close in colour to Caen stone in order to match the ancient fabric of the abbey. Even then not everyone could be concealed completely or camouflaged in this way, and so – in much the same way that early newscasters were required to wear black tie even on the wireless – one of the BBC men who found himself crouched in a more exposed position was required to wear full morning dress complete with gloves and medals.

On the big day even the relative stars of the broadcasting world were warned to expect little in the way of special privileges, so that Richard Dimbleby – having bunked down the previous night in a barge moored on the opposite bank of the river – rowed a dinghy across the Thames on Coronation Day morning. His reasons for doing so were eminently sensible, to avoid being caught up in the heavy traffic which every Londoner knows; but dressed in tailcoat and top hat he must have cut an extraordinary figure for anyone out and about early enough to catch him at it.

Official court photographer Cecil Beaton was similarly told he would be confined to a tiny 'rook's nest' up in the gods, reaching this modest perch via a winding staircase where he found that 'the iced wind blew in circles . . . and I felt much sympathy for Hunt'. (News had just reached London that Lord Hunt's expedition to conquer Everest had been successful.) Squeezed in among organ pipes, he took his mind off the discomfort by sharing a ration of barley sugar with Christopher Hussey of *Country Life*.

Despite the sheer volume of William Walton's 'Orb And Sceptre' issuing from the pipes once proceedings began, Beaton was able to concentrate sufficiently to make some detailed sketches of the velvet and ermine-clad congregation down below. Never exactly a soul of discretion, he cruelly (but characteristically) recalled 'the bald spots of the peeresses' and a member of the nobility surreptitiously 'nipping from a flask', yet admitted in his diary that they were overall a 'ravishing sight, like a bed of auricula-eyed Sweet William in their red velvet and foam-white, dew-spangled with diamonds.'

Away from the abbey the technicians and backroom boys were frantically busy too, with two shifts on duty simultaneously at the BBC's

The Royal Arms in Regent Street.

Alexandra Palace in north London. A special edition of the *Radio Times* was produced (this was to sell more than nine million copies) and yet more Corporation staff were stationed at the nearby Kays Film Laboratory in Finsbury Park, beavering away in the darkroom processing film. The chief task was loading huge film magazines from the new Suppressed Frame Telerecording system, a device developed by the BBC's own research department and installed at 'A.P.' specifically for the Coronation Day broadcasts. Each magazine held 1,000ft of 35mm film, which following the live transmission was edited for a later, evening broadcast[*].

Of course for millions of viewers at home the fruits of all this effort began much earlier in the day, at 10.15 when what was to be a genuinely historic television broadcast commenced with the voice of a female continuity announcer. 'This is the BBC Television Service,' Miss Sylvia Peters began:

> Good morning everyone. This is a great and joyous day for us all. In a few minutes our queen starts on her journey from Buckingham Palace to Westminster Abbey, there to be crowned Queen Elizabeth the second. But it is not only a day of rejoicing, for underlying the abbey ceremonies and the splendid pageantry of the many processions is the deep significance of the simple fact that the Queen is today dedicating herself before God to the service of her subjects.

Not unreasonably the BBC wished also to highlight its own special role in the proceedings, and so – notwithstanding the fact that everyone in the country must already have known this – Ms Peters[**] continued, saying:

> For the first time in history through the medium of television the ancient and noble rite of a coronation service will be witnessed by millions of Her Majesty's subjects. As we watch them here, these

The Ministry of Defence stands sentinel.

television pictures will be relayed across the Channel to many thousands of viewers in France, Holland and Germany, including members of Her Majesty's Forces serving in those countries. From now until after five o'clock this afternoon television cameras will be taking you into the heart of London to watch and to share in each phase of this great day's events.

Sixteen months after the late king's sad and premature death, and following the most intensive programme of planning, organisation and painstaking rehearsal, the big day had finally begun.

---

[*]   In a digital age it is interesting to note that around 80,000ft of cinematography film was used by the BBC on the day of the coronation. Recordings for radio broadcast similarly required an incredible 3,400 12in disks together with 250 disks of other sizes and some 200 reels – equivalent to more than 85 miles – of magnetic tape.

[**]   Originally a musical actress, in 1947 Peters answered a newspaper advertisement and went on to become one of the Corporation's first continuity announcers. She remained at the BBC until the late 1950s during which time she coached Her Majesty the Queen in the necessary broadcasting skills required to make the annual Christmas telecasts.

Whitehall again, it's never looked finer.

6

HER MAJESTY'S GOWN

Without wishing to diminish in any way the herculean effort and expertise which went into planning the coronation, or to minimise the manpower involved in remodelling the abbey and planning and executing the processions to and from Westminster, it must have been obvious almost from the moment of the late king's death that for many observers the single most important item on the day would be the queen's choice of dress.

Clearly any such garment had to be not simply striking and beautiful and authentically majestic, but also comfortable and practical. Practical, that is, in the sense that it should be designed and constructed in such a way that the wearer could move around without difficulty and spend a long and fairly arduous day fastened into it. Most obviously it was also essential that the dress should stand out on the day, and not disappear into the background of ermine and velvet and tiaras worn by the peers and peeresses gathered in the abbey.

The Queen Mother was naturally on hand to lend her own advice about what was appropriate for such an occasion, and her experience was invaluable. For a relatively young woman Her Majesty was also very sure of her own opinions, however, and very early on selected Norman Hartnell for the task and asked him to design something in white satin. It was to be regal and religious, follow the broad outline of her wedding gown and to be as timeless as the coronation service itself.

As her chosen British designer, Hartnell was a shrewd choice and far from unexpected. A Royal Warrant Holder since 1940 – as dressmaker 'by Appointment' to HM The Queen Mother – he

was Cambridge-educated despite somewhat humble origins (his father was a publican). After abandoning his degree and a brief but unsuccessful acting career, he had very quickly become established at premises in Bruton Street, Mayfair, with an enviable clientele. (By happy chance this was the very same street in which his new sovereign had been born.)

Mindful of the queen's firm preferences, Hartnell[*] set out to carefully and thoroughly research the history of English coronation gowns. His own experience was limited, in that for the 1937 coronation he had been responsible for the maids of honours' dresses but not that of the queen herself. Using the archives of the Museum of London, however, and the extensive resources of the private London Library in St James's Square, he was soon able to refine his ideas and before long, his mind buzzing with thoughts of heraldic emblems and sparkling gemstones, he produced a series of eight paintings to illustrate to the queen the direction of his thinking.

Ranging from the simple and severe to highly elaborate pieces of costume theatre replete with religious images and overtones, the eight were presented to Her Majesty as the starting point for long and involved discussions. Particular favourites were reportedly numbers six and eight, although the latter with its silver and crystal themes was felt to be too close to her wedding gown and so was rejected. Number six,

---

[*] He was knighted in time for the 1977 Silver Jubilee, the first couturier so honoured.

Thousands of troops …

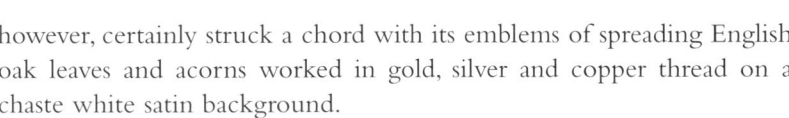
… from all over the Commonwealth …

however, certainly struck a chord with its emblems of spreading English oak leaves and acorns worked in gold, silver and copper thread on a chaste white satin background.

Over time elements of the eighth made a return, but with colour tints to differentiate it from Her Majesty's wedding gown (and indeed from that worn by the unmarried Victoria at her own coronation). Further refinements were also made at the suggestion of the Duke of Edinburgh, in particular to incorporate surface designs which were emblematic of the Commonwealth and Dominions as well as of the United Kingdom – reflecting the queen's genuinely international role as sovereign.

For England the obvious emblem to choose was a Tudor Rose, for Scotland the thistle which was worked in pale mauve silk and amethysts, and a pale green shamrock represented Ireland. Wales briefly posed a bit of a problem, Hartnell objecting to the leek on aesthetic grounds but being refused permission (by the Garter King of Arms) to swap it for a yellow daffodil. Eventually the two compromised by softening the vegetable's colour, the leek being embroidered in white and pale green silk and enhanced by diamante. The other emblems included the Canadian maple leaf, the Australian wattle flower, a New Zealand fern, the South African protea, also known as the sugarbush and created in pink silk with silver-bordered leaves. For India there was the Lotus flower, with a complex arrangement of wheat, jute and cotton for her neighbour Pakistan,

Needless to say the colour selection for all this was critically important too, and the decision process very time consuming. Like Her Majesty's make-up and that of her attendants, which naturally required another round of discussions, the preferred hues had not only to work in daylight but also to look at their best in the soft pinkish surroundings of the state coach as well as under the harsh yellow lighting required by the cameras of the BBC to light the normally hushed and subdued interior of the ancient abbey.

Once the design was finally agreed, however, work on the dress itself was able to begin in earnest and great secrecy, with three seamstresses and six embroiderers working on bolts of luxurious white satin. (This had originated from the same Lullingstone Castle silk mill in Kent which had produced the material for the queen's wedding dress as well as her mother's coronation gown.) As early as Christmas 1952 the dress was ready for a first fitting, its construction as much a piece of engineering as dressmaking with, for example, pads and multiple layers of horsehair backing the silk in order to disperse the weight of the heavy, jewelled skirt and to ensure that the gown hung correctly.

… and tens of thousands who came to applaud them.

At Buckingham Palace, meanwhile, the queen and her six maids of honour were engaged in yet more rehearsals of the scenes that lay ahead. In particular the six[*] were to spend many hours with a piece of fabric representing the crimson velvet robe (see Chapter 4): holding and folding it, walking and pausing, and practicing entering and leaving a mock-up of the state coach which palace staff had built using a number of chairs. (The genuine robe, attached to the shoulders, was edged with ermine and two rows of delicately embroidered gold lace and gold filigree.) For at least one rehearsal the Imperial State Crown was quietly

removed to Buckingham Palace, the queen sensibly deciding to wear the 7lb behemoth for almost an entire day in order better to understand its shape, weight and balance.

Determined to make the most of the time allowed him, Hartnell personally delivered the completed gown to the palace with just three days to spare, the queen pronouncing it 'glorious' and requiring no more alterations. In fact the finished garment had travelled up the Mall by van, with its creator travelling in a car behind 'to keep an eye on it'. (He had also, secretly, included one additional piece of embroidery on the left-hand side of the gown, a tiny four-leafed shamrock for luck which the queen's hand would brush past several times during the day of the ceremony[**].)

---

[*]   Personally selected by Her Majesty the six were: Lady Mary Baillie-Hamilton, daughter of the 12th Earl of Haddington; Lady Jane Vane-Tempest-Stewart, daughter of the 8th Marquess of Londonderry; Lady Jane Heathcote-Drummond-Willoughby, daughter of the 27th Baron Willoughby De Eresby and 3rd Earl of Ancaster; Lady Anne Coke, daughter of the 5th Earl of Leicester; Lady Rosemary Spencer-Churchill, daughter of the 10th Duke of Marlborough; and Lady Moyra Hamilton, daughter of the 4th Duke of Abercorn.

[**]   The dress has since been worn just six times: for receptions at Buckingham Palace and the Palace of Holyroodhouse; and at the Opening of Parliament in New Zealand, Australia and Ceylon (in 1954) and in Canada three years later.

Those in open carriages braved the rain …

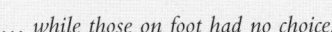

… while those on foot had no choice.

7

Into the Abbey

As the day of the coronation drew closer the sense of expectation and excitement was palpable, and so infectious as to touch people in both Britain and abroad regardless of their sex, age, politics or class. Evidently this was as true of the invited guests as it was for the general public, and just as many hours of film footage and tens of thousands of photographs exist to show the streets thronging with a happy multitude so the published diaries of the time bear witness to the enthusiasm and anticipation among the normally insouciant Establishment and upper classes.

Always lively and engaging, the diaries of the politician and socialite Sir Henry 'Chips' Channon, for example, suggest an aristocracy thrown into happy convulsions by the rare excitement of what was about to unfold. In a confusion of what he calls 'coaches and robes, tiaras and decorations' we learn that the 'Marchioness of Londonderry has a carriage but no horses', that 'the Duchess of Buccleuch has horses but no positillion to lead them', and that 'the Countess of Portarlington ("Winnie") can muster no more than a harness'.

Admittedly other members of the aristocracy were somewhat better equipped, but often they fared no better either. Worst of all, in Wilton Crescent the night before, the Belgravia home of the Duke and Duchess of Sutherland was burgled – at a cost to the His Grace of £30,000 worth of diamonds (or £50,000, depending on which newspaper one read). And while Their Graces the Duke and Duchess of Devonshire were well provided for in terms of jewels, horses, a carriage and a postillion, things went so wrong in the planning department that their ensemble got lost on the way to the abbey. (This might have had something to do with the means of communication between the duke and his coachman, directions being communicated to the poor man via a piece of string tied to one of the buttons on his livery.)

Inevitably even among the grandest of grandees not everyone could aspire to an inheritance of such luxuries, however, and for the benefit of the more impecunious peers and parliamentarians the capital's Transport Executive (lineal ancestor of our own Transport for London) agreed to lay on special trains from High Street Kensington to the old Westminster underground station. Elsewhere the traffic was bumper to bumper from very early in the morning, Beaton again enjoying himself observing everyone getting into a state as he made his way back to his rook's nest. This time it was the occupants of taxis which caught his eye, ordinarily important personages trapped and going nowhere, 'the old men, bad tempered and sleepy at this hour, in cockaded hats with lace jabots, their womenfolk having had, before dawn, a hairdresser to their homes to set their *coiffures*.'

For privileged observers inside the abbey the view was a similar mix of prestige and confusion, incredible grandeur and ordinary, everyday detail. Diarist James Lees-Milne, seated within sight of St Edward's Chair but not the altar, took a certain waspish pleasure counting in the grandees while thinking their coronets looked absurd. Wearing his at a 'scornful tilt' the 7th Duke of Wellington was likened to a dowager, while the 28th Earl of Balcarres and Crawford, Lees-Milne thought, looked 'roguish'. Overall, he felt, 'the robes and uniforms with their depths of colour

The special guests started to take their places in the stands.

and glitter of gold were far too splendid for most of the wearers.' Also shocking was how very many of the peers were bald, although the diaries identify a few glamorous exceptions among the ladies such as Lady Euston, the future Duchess of Grafton ('a Rhinemaiden') and the 'most striking' Dowager Duchess of Devonshire with her 'enormous diamond tiara, small coronet and a train of infinite length'.

What effect such a display made on the foreign dignitaries and heads of state is not recorded, but naturally they were there in great numbers too, Cecil Beaton enjoying the procession of what he termed 'minor Royalties,' many of course related to the queen, and from as far afield as Norway, Greece, Nepal, Japan, Ethiopia, Thailand and Peru. Joining

them were the 'Sultans under Her Majesty's protection', and the fabulous Queen of Tonga, Salote Toupu III, on whose 'great big warm personality' the press fastened to the lasting delight of the British public[*]. (At the opposite end of the scale, perhaps, was the Duke of Edinburgh's mother,

---

[*] On seeing the Tongan ruler, and her diminutive husband Chief Viliami Tungī Mailefihi, Noel Coward is widely reported to have quipped 'Oh, that's her lunch' when asked by Princess Marina, Duchess of Kent who the gentleman was. However, while enjoying the anecdote – a more light-hearted one than it might now appear – Coward always denied he had said such a thing, insisting that the joke had actually originated at the bar of the venerable White's club in St James's.

a slightly shadowy figure and dressed, in contrast to the pageantry and grandeur all around her, in the 'ash-grey draperies of a nun'.)

For the those not able to gain access to the abbey, however – not to mention the millions watching at home – the chief interest at this point still lay outside Westminster Abbey and in the first great procession as the royal party and its attendants made their way toward the great church. They did so under the scrutiny of more than 100 microphones positioned along the relatively short route and countless television and film cameras. (A second much longer route was planned for the return journey after the coronation, giving Londoners a better opportunity to glimpse their new queen as she made her way back to the palace.)

For public and broadcasters alike the proceedings thus began at Buckingham Palace itself. Here the BBC had installed its microphones and recording equipment in a room overlooking the main quadrangle, and scores of palace staff and servants had assembled to see the queen's departure. Radio and television commentators were positioned at the Queen Victoria Memorial in front of the palace, and more of them at the end of the Mall where the curved stone of Sir Aston Webb's Admiralty Arch marks the junction with Trafalgar Square. Crossing along the bottom of the square the procession then passed down Northumberland Avenue to Victoria Embankment where more than 30,000 places had been reserved especially for children from London to observe the proceedings[*]. The sight which greeted them was one never seen before, and not yet equalled, a riot of gold and bright colours, horses and uniforms, pageantry and splendour of precisely the kind at which this country has traditionally excelled.

The queen, with the Duke of Edinburgh, was to travel in the Gold State Coach, a magnificent mid-eighteenth-century device more than 24ft-long and half as high. Built by Samuel Butler in 1762, a liveryman of the Worshipful Company of Coachmakers and Coach Harness Makers, it has been used for every coronation since that of George IV. On this

And the procession began.

occasion it was to be pulled by eight grey geldings from the Royal Mews – Tovey, Tedder, Cunningham, Noah, Eisenhower, Snow White, Tipperary and McCreery – and has since been used only twice, for Her Majesty's Silver and Golden Jubilees.

For the journey Her Majesty wore the George IV State Diadem – the smaller crown she is shown wearing on stamps and coins[**] – the Duke of Edinburgh being arrayed in the full-dress uniform of the Royal Navy (although in the abbey itself this was covered by his duke's robe worn under a coronet). The queen also carried a special coronation bouquet, all-white and comprising orchids and lilies-of-the-valley from England, stephanotis from Scotland, and carnations from Northern Ireland and the Isle of Man, with additional orchids from Wales.

But while the Gold State Coach remains without doubt the finest such vehicle in the country – eclipsing even that of the Lord Mayor of London, which has similar painted allegorical panels by Giovanni Battista

---

[*] Very special arrangements were in place for around 34,000 children, and more than half a century later Dorothy Kendall, a widow from Tullibody, Clackmannanshire, recalled her time as a WPC helping to police the area set aside for them on the Embankment. She told the *Daily Mail*, 'there was music playing from early morning and the whole atmosphere was wonderful. I can still hear the cheering as the children waved their banners until their arms ached. I would love to have waved too but I had to stand to attention as each carriage went past'. Later in the day, she recalled, vans arrived with thousands of ice creams and cartons of juice with straws, which the police then handed out to the youngsters.

[**] This should in no way suggest the diadem is a modest item. Created in 1820 for George IV's coronation, it incorporates various national symbols – including roses, shamrocks and thistles – as well as 1,333 diamonds and 169 pearls. It is usually on display at the Queen's Gallery at Buckingham Palace.

At times the procession seemed to outnumber the spectators …

… as the marchers just kept on coming.

Cipriani, but only six horses – it was only one of many taking part in the lengthy procession. Before Her Majesty had even left Buckingham Palace many more carriages were already beginning their journey, all of them drawn from the royal collection which is known to number more than 100 such vehicles. Among the first were four conveying colonial rulers such as the Sultans of Zanzibar, Brunei and Johore. A further nine carried the Prime Minister Sir Winston Churchill and his opposite numbers from Canada, Australia and New Zealand, South Africa, India and Pakistan, Northern Ireland and Southern Rhodesia[*].

There were of course many of our own royals in the carriage procession too, with three carriages being provided for the princes and princesses of royal blood. Impressively these included several for whom this would have been their fourth coronation, such as Her Highness Princess Marie Louise, a granddaughter of Queen Victoria, who had been present in the abbey in 1902 for Edward VII, in 1911 for George V, and again in May 1937 for the queen's father, King George VI. Prince Charles was also en route to Westminster by this time, the first English child ever to witness the coronation of his mother, but sadly not Princess Anne, who was considered too young to attend. (Nor the ailing Queen Mary, Queen Dowager who at eighty-one became the first queen to see a grandchild ascend to the throne but passed away just ten weeks prior to her coronation.) Finally of course, there was Queen Elizabeth the Queen Mother, the late king's much loved widow, bringing up the rear of the carriages in a glass coach with her daughter, Princess Margaret.

Lesser figures travelled to the abbey by motor car[**], a procession of gleaming black and claret limousines carrying foreign royals and other heads of state as well as what at the time were documented merely as 'Certain Members of the Royal Family'. These would have included the likes of the Earl and Countess of Harewood (she was George V's only daughter), the Marchioness of Milford Haven and Countess Mountbatten of Burma. Society's most blue-blooded members, in other words, if not by modern standards individuals necessarily identified as being royal. This being England there was also an ambulance bringing up the rear, a facility which was provided (as Vita Sackville-West's journalist husband Harold Nicolson wryly noted) 'for any horses that might get hurt'.

For Londoners and indeed television viewers it would have been a truly spectacular sight, one contrasting strongly with the drabness and austerity of the post-war years and something which goes a long way to explaining the more than three million people who poured onto the streets to see it. The atmosphere was respectful but almost carnival-like, and this too would have been in marked contrast to the sombre nature of the events about to unfold within the ancient walls of Westminster Abbey.

Aside from those actually taking part in the procession, those fortunate enough to witness the coronation in person had to be seated surprisingly early – hence the sandwiches, presumably – the doors to the abbey being closed at 8.30 prompt. This was done in order to ensure that everyone was in place by the time the first of the dignitaries started arriving – cars first, then carriages – and it was almost eleven o'clock before Her Majesty appeared and entered the building. As noted earlier she was assisted by her six maids of honour, each dressed lily-like in white satin embroidered with pearl blossoms and discreet trails of small golden leaves. They were responsible for carrying the heavy 18ft-long Robe of State attached to the queen's shoulders, and for removing it in preparation for the ceremony.

In simple terms a coronation service falls into six discrete parts: the recognition, the oath, the anointing, the investiture – this stage includes the actual crowning – the enthronement and the homage. London in 1953 was to be no different.

The ceremony began to the sound of 'I Was Glad', a resounding setting of Psalm 122 by Sir Hubert Parry, for a long time the preeminent composer for such occasions. Then, with the Queen's Scholars from neighbouring Westminster School proclaiming loudly 'Vivat Regina! Vivat Regina Elizabeth! Vivat! Vivat! Vivat!', the central figure standing before St Edward's Chair turned first to the east, then to the south, west and north, allowing her people to see her and literally to recognise her as their new sovereign.

As she did so, and in a fine piece of theatre, Archbishop Geoffrey Fisher, the Lord High Chancellor of Great Britain, the Lord Great Chamberlain of England, the Lord High Constable of England and the Earl Marshal each bore witness as the Garter Principal King of Arms four times demanded of the audience: 'Sirs, I here present unto you Queen Elizabeth, your undoubted Queen: wherefore all you who are come this day to do your homage and service, are you willing to do the same?' From each point of the compass came the response 'God save Queen Elizabeth', to which the new queen deeply bowed.

---

[*]   In all a total of 129 nations and territories were officially represented at the coronation service.

[**]   Many of these, together with the Gold State Coach and other carriages, were parked around the corner in Dean's Yard while the queen and the congregation filed into the abbey.

Swearing the coronation oath was a longer process, administered by the Archbishop and with the queen swearing to govern each of her realms according to their respective laws and customs. Also to mete out law and justice with mercy, to protect the Church of England and preserve its bishops and clergy, and to uphold the established religion of this country. Finishing with the words, 'The things which I have here promised, I will perform, and keep. So help me God' the queen then kissed the Bible and returned it to the Dean of Westminster. In a change from tradition the Dean then handed it back, explaining that this was 'to keep your Majesty ever mindful of the Law and Gospel of God as the rule for the whole life and government of Christian princes'.

Following the Creed and Communion service another piece of theatre is required, in which to the sound of G.F. Handel's 'Zadok the Priest'* the sovereign is traditionally divested of all jewels and finery, these being replaced or covered by a simple white linen garment. Thus arrayed, the queen then moved towards St Edward's Chair and, while seated, was anointed on the hands, heart and breast by the Archbishop of Canterbury using holy oil.

It will be recalled that this part of the ceremony was regarded as absolutely central to the coronation and thus sacrosanct, a silk canopy being used to conceal proceedings from the television viewers and from those watching at home. As a result it remains one of the most

---

* Taken from the Book of Kings the words of this striking hymn have formed part of the Coronation Service since 973 and the crowing of King Edgar. In 1727 Handel set them to music for George III and they have been used in this form ever since.

mysterious elements of British ceremonial, something witnessed only by the participants and the four Knights of the Garter supporting the canopy. In fact the very notion of holy oil has these days such a ring of 'magick' to it, a sense of the occult, that few even trouble to ask what it actually comprises. Fewer still could answer such a question, although it is known that at the coronation of Charles I the oil used included orange, jasmine, distilled roses, distilled cinnamon, oil of ben – a relation of the horseradish – extract of bensoint, ambergris, musk and civet. In 1953 a slightly simpler recipe is thought to have been used, comprising oils of orange, roses, cinnamon, musk and ambergris.

Once this part of the ceremony was complete, and the canopy removed, the queen was dressed in two unique items of clothing, the plain linen Colobium Sindonis and her own father's gold Supertunica (or Dalmatica). Relatively humble garments, the pair is intended to remind the sovereign that power is derived from the people.

Once dressed in this way the queen returned to the coronation chair where she was invested with the regalia. Some items, such as the Orb, are presented symbolically and then returned to the altar. Likewise the golden spurs, and the Sword of State. But others she retained, including a ring[*] – the 'Wedding Ring of England' – and the Sceptre with the Cross and the Sceptre with the Dove (symbolising sovereign power and justice and mercy). These she held in her hands. Now at last, with the Archbishop receiving St Edward's Crown from the Dean of Westminster, came the moment of the actual coronation[**].

As observed by Cecil Beaton from his perch among the pipes, this enormously symbolic act was 'superbly dramatic: the expression on the small face of the Queen one of extreme expectancy until, with magnificent assurance, the Archbishop thrusts down with speed and force the Crown on the neat head.' Simultaneously, trumpet fanfares echoed down the great nave, the congregation acclaimed the sovereign with loud and repeated shouts, and a few miles downriver, at the Tower of London,

a twenty-one-gun salute sounded out across London. It was exciting but also, for James Lees-Milne, 'very moving, the young Queen so calm, grave and sure of every movement, and so palpably serious and intent.'

For Lees-Milne and the others privileged to be seated inside the abbey – and privileged not just because the weather outside was 'damnable' – there were many such moving memories to take away. These included the queen's self-evident humility during the service itself, her poise throughout what was to be a very long day, and also the very rare sight – never since repeated – of Elizabeth as sovereign curtseying, not once but four times, as she turned to the congregation and was recognised at each point of the compass.

With the benediction read, and Elizabeth seated in the throne, the last acts of the service saw the Archbishop of Canterbury and the other bishops offering her their fealty, and behind them the royal dukes – Edinburgh, Gloucester and Kent – and the peers, in strict order of precedence, paying homage and allegiance to their new queen. For 'Chips' Channon – an American – the coronation service had seemed endless, and yet paradoxically 'the scene was so splendid, so breathtaking in its solemn splendour that it passed in a flash.'

And now it was over. Following a cry of 'God save Queen Elizabeth. Long live Queen Elizabeth. May the Queen live for ever,' and as the assembled thousands filled the abbey with the words of the National Anthem, Elizabeth, now wearing the Imperial State Crown and holding the Sceptre with the Cross and the Orb, left the Collegiate Church of St Peter, the scene of an extraordinary thirty-nine coronations, and stepped back into the world.

---

[*] The ring dates back to the coronation of King William IV in 1831. Made at a cost of £157, it takes the form of a sapphire surmounted by a cross in rubies surrounded by diamonds. It has been worn at every coronation since, excepting that of Queen Victoria whose fingers were too small.

[**] Made in 1661, St Edward's Crown is of solid gold and weighs 4lb 12oz. In its current form it was first used by Charles II, as it had to be redesigned after the Restoration using elements of an older crown. There is speculation that the lower part might be from Edward the Confessor's own crown, but this is by no means certain.

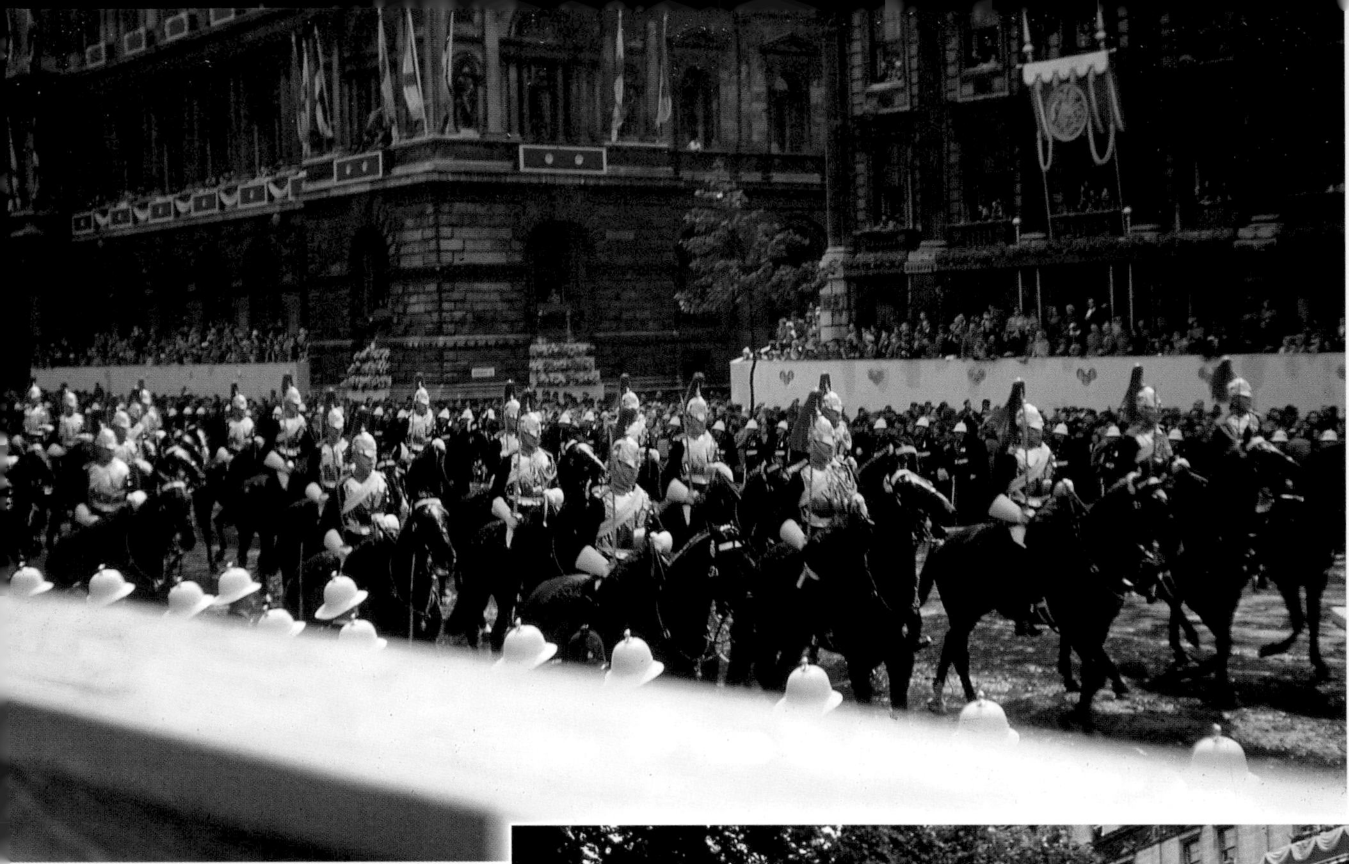

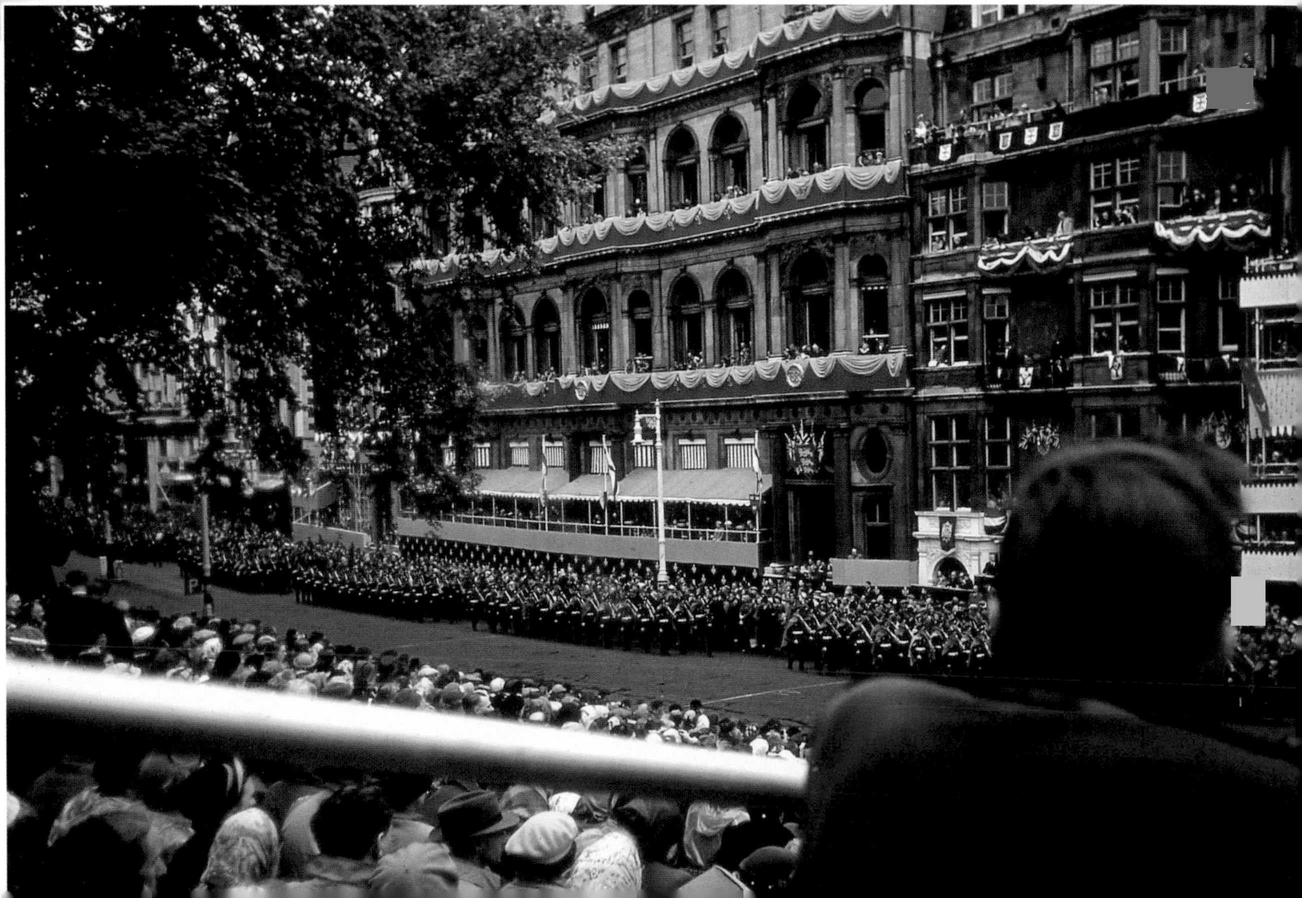

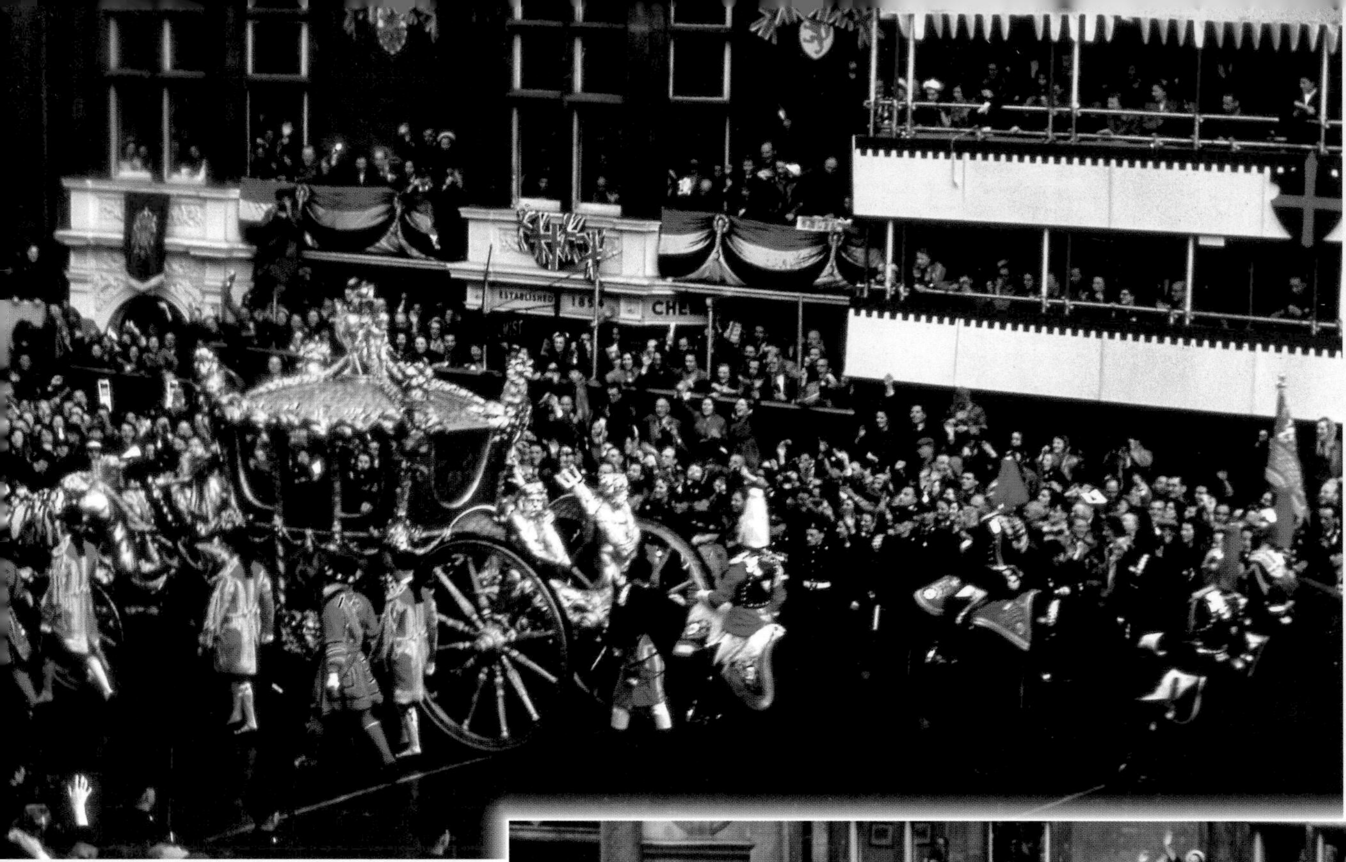
ESTABLISHED

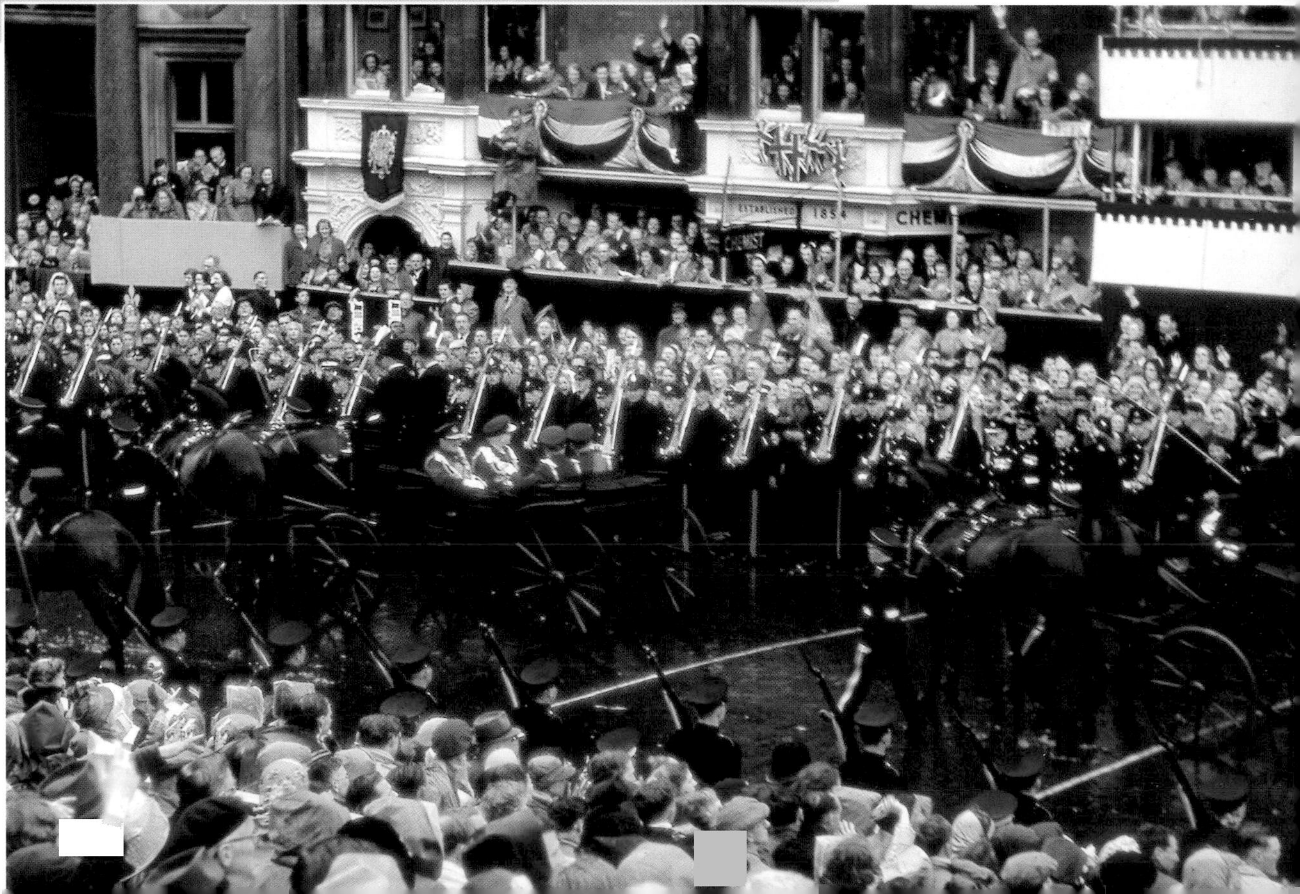
ESTABLISHED
CHEMIST

In its element: the Household Cavalry.

8

REJOINING LONDON

Outside in the streets, the weather was indeed utterly damnable. Much of May had been glorious, with several weeks of warmth and sunshine interspersed with only the occasional, brief thundery downpour. Eight days before Coronation Day, and notwithstanding the fact that it was a bank holiday, the temperature in the south-east had peaked at 31.7°C. But by the second day of June normal service had been resumed: in London, caught between a high pressure area over the Atlantic and an area of low pressure over the continent, it rained all day – and once the processions were underway it positively poured.

In the comfort of the Travellers' Club in Pall Mall, diarist Harold Nicolson and his fellow members enjoyed 'an excellent luncheon' before going to 'our places on the stand [one of several erected around the 5½-mile route]. Guardsmen wait in front of us and the rain pours down on their bearskins.' Around the corner in St James's Street the wet, upward slope of the road towards Piccadilly was enough to defeat the hooves and gun carriages of the Royal Horse Artillery, and everywhere people on the pavement – civilians as well as many thousands of military personnel – were getting drenched.

In contrast to the procession from palace to abbey which had been reasonably direct, the more circuitous return route was carefully planned to take in much of London's West End. This would give as many people as possible an opportunity to enjoy the colour and pageantry of the occasion, and of course to glimpse their new queen.

By early morning several million were lining the route as it took in Whitehall, Trafalgar Square and Pall Mall before passing by the sovereign's

official London residence at St James's Palace. At least on Piccadilly the French arcade beneath the Ritz Hotel would have afforded some of the spectators cover as the cars and carriages made their way through the rain towards Apsley House, the old Duke of Wellington's townhouse at Hyde Park Corner. From there, after travelling the length of Park Lane, the procession was to turn along Oxford Street to Oxford Circus, then take another right down Regent Street to Piccadilly Circus, and through more

The procession at Hyde Park Corner.

Hyde Park corner in the rain …

… but spirits remained high.

rain along the Haymarket and back into Trafalgar Square. Passing beneath Admiralty Arch and along the Mall, the queen and her attendants would then return to Buckingham Palace for a keenly anticipated appearance on Aston Webb's famous balcony and the aforementioned flypast[*].

At a time when intercontinental travel was far from the norm and horribly expensive, surprising numbers of those watching from the pavements had come from overseas. When a television reporter set out to interview some of the spectators waving union flags he found an Australian family who had sailed halfway around the globe in a little ketch to be part of history, and an Alpine guide who had just arrived from republican Switzerland. In a way with which we are now entirely familiar others had camped overnight – sometimes two nights – just to be sure of securing the most favourable vantage points from which to enjoy the day.

Few would have known at that time – or probably cared – that inside the abbey things had not gone quite as smoothly as had been hoped. Despite the many months of planning and all the rehearsals, the queen was to experience her own little coronation glitches, as for instance when wire from the gold lace on her mantel became caught up in the new abbey carpet. In such weighty apparel this made it hard for her to move forward at all, let alone gracefully. Realising at once what had happened she whispered, 'get me moving' to the Archbishop of Canterbury, the startled prelate giving Her Majesty a firm but polite shove to see her on her way. Later on she also had not so much to forge her own signature as to fake it, when it was discovered that the official inkwell was dry. At least, when it mattered, the crown had been placed on her head the right way round, possibly it was said afterwards because a farsighted courtier had placed a small gold star on the inside of the rim in order that the Archbishop could tell the front from the back.

But outside in the rain such things were trifles and of no account. London was in the mood for a long overdue celebration and nothing – not the rain, not the cold, and certainly not the dry inkwell of a dusty

Tiered seating conceals St George's Hospital.

---

[*]   Her Majesty actually made several appearances with her family on the famous balcony, but only once greeted the immense, cheering crowds wearing the Imperial State Crown and the Royal Robes. She appeared for the final time at around 9.45 p.m. to turn on the celebratory 'Lights of London'. These were illuminations cascading down the Mall and lighting a huge cipher on Admiralty Arch. In Trafalgar Square at the same time more lights 'turned the fountains to liquid silver' while floodlights illuminated the National Gallery. The Tower of London – strictly speaking still a royal palace – was also lit in this way.

cleric – was going to stand in its way. As the queen emerged from the abbey the streets around erupted with a joyous cacophony of cheering and whistles and applause, and for a while nothing else mattered.

Momentarily the sun shone as the Gold State Coach turned into Parliament Square, but by then most of the spectators were simply too wet for the weather to matter. Already soaked through, civilians and soldiers alike knew their options were limited, and instead of cowering from the rain even those who might have found shelter crowded forward to see as much of the proceedings as they could. Clearly some of the dignitaries took the same sensible view, and sixty years later one suspects that much of the Queen of Tonga's huge popular appeal lay in her refusal to draw the hood of her carriage. Instead, and like the people who wished to see who was in the procession, she let the rain fall on her – and *que sera sera*. (In fact the only damage she sustained was to a plume of red feathers, a tiny thing compared to the roars of approval from the pavement as her carriage hove into view.)

In the vastly more splendid Gold State Coach the queen was now wearing the weighty Imperial State Crown, decorated with three large pearls traditionally believed – and this has not been disproved – to have once been been the earrings of Good Queen Bess. Beneath it she was dressed in the new Purple Robe of Estate, a sumptuous garment edged with ermine and a heavily embroidered border of gold. (Together with the embroidered royal cipher, the border – of wheat ears and olive branches – was reported to have taken team of twelve seamstresses from the Royal School of Needlework a total of 3,500 hours to complete.)

For others involved in the procession, such as the lead troopers of the Household Cavalry, the overwhelming impression was one of noise: rousing music from the military bands, more than 5 miles of cheering spectators on either side of the route and – in the absence of any means of mobile communications – orders barked at them from the Army's tannoys which were strung along the way. The decorations too were extraordinary by the standards of the time, with seemingly the whole city bedecked with colourful banners and crowns. Among the best were many famous landmarks such as the Selfridges department store and Eros in his illuminated, gilded cage; but thousands of private homeowners had joined in too, while on the Thames many of the boats and barges moored midstream had rigged up strings of flags and lights in a way which had rarely if ever been seen before.

Approaching Buckingham Palace, looking happy, radiant and quite beautiful, the queen was greeted by tens of thousands of voices along the Mall all singing the National Anthem as this was played by a band in the courtyard of the palace. Passing through the gates at approximately 4.30 p.m., many hours after the Gold State Coach had first left, the newly crowned queen was about to meet her people.

Outside, the crowds pressed towards the gates much as they had last done on VE Day in 1945, massing around the Victoria Memorial and pushing up against the black and gold railings to witness the by-now familiar balcony appearance. They had a wait, but at around 5.15, still wearing the Imperial State Crown and looking every bit as delighted as the hundreds of thousands of people thronging down below, the queen stepped outside accompanied by her husband the Duke of Edinburgh and their two children. As the crowd roared their approval they were joined by Her Majesty the Queen Mother, by Princess Margaret and other members of the royal family as well as Her Majesty's pages and maids of honour.

Violent thunderstorms over the Thames estuary unfortunately delayed the flypast but after a few minutes – with royal fingers pointing at the sky to alert the young Prince Charles and his sister to what was happening – the show began, the first of more than 160 British and Canadian jet aircraft winging their way in low over the West End. Their controller, Air Vice-Marshal Lord Bandon, talked the flights in one by one, from his temporary command post on the palace roof.

Thereafter the queen and Prince Philip made several returns to the balcony during the course of the early evening, acknowledging the almost continuous cheering from below, the crowds swelling as more and more people flooded into the Mall from their positions on the processional route. After making a radio address to the Nation and Commonwealth at 9 p.m. (the text of which follows) Her Majesty made her final appearance outside on the balcony. Now dressed in an evening gown and once more wearing the George IV State Diadem, she and the duke were able to enjoy the acclamation of her people and the best possible vantage point to witness the vast firework display which now exploded over the River Thames.

Coronation Day was over – a spectacle witnessed personally by millions and remotely by tens of millions more – and the New Elizabethan Era could truly be said to have begun.

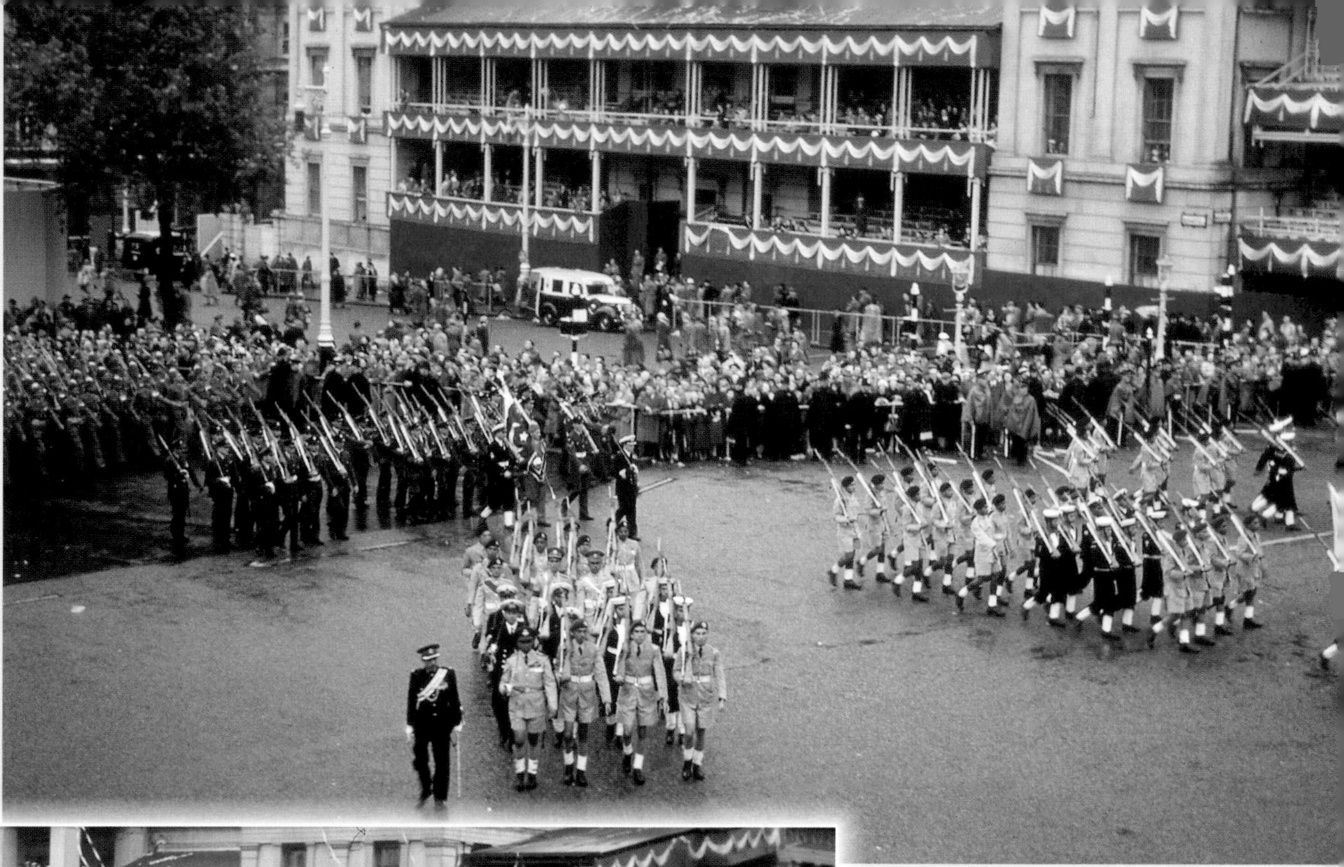

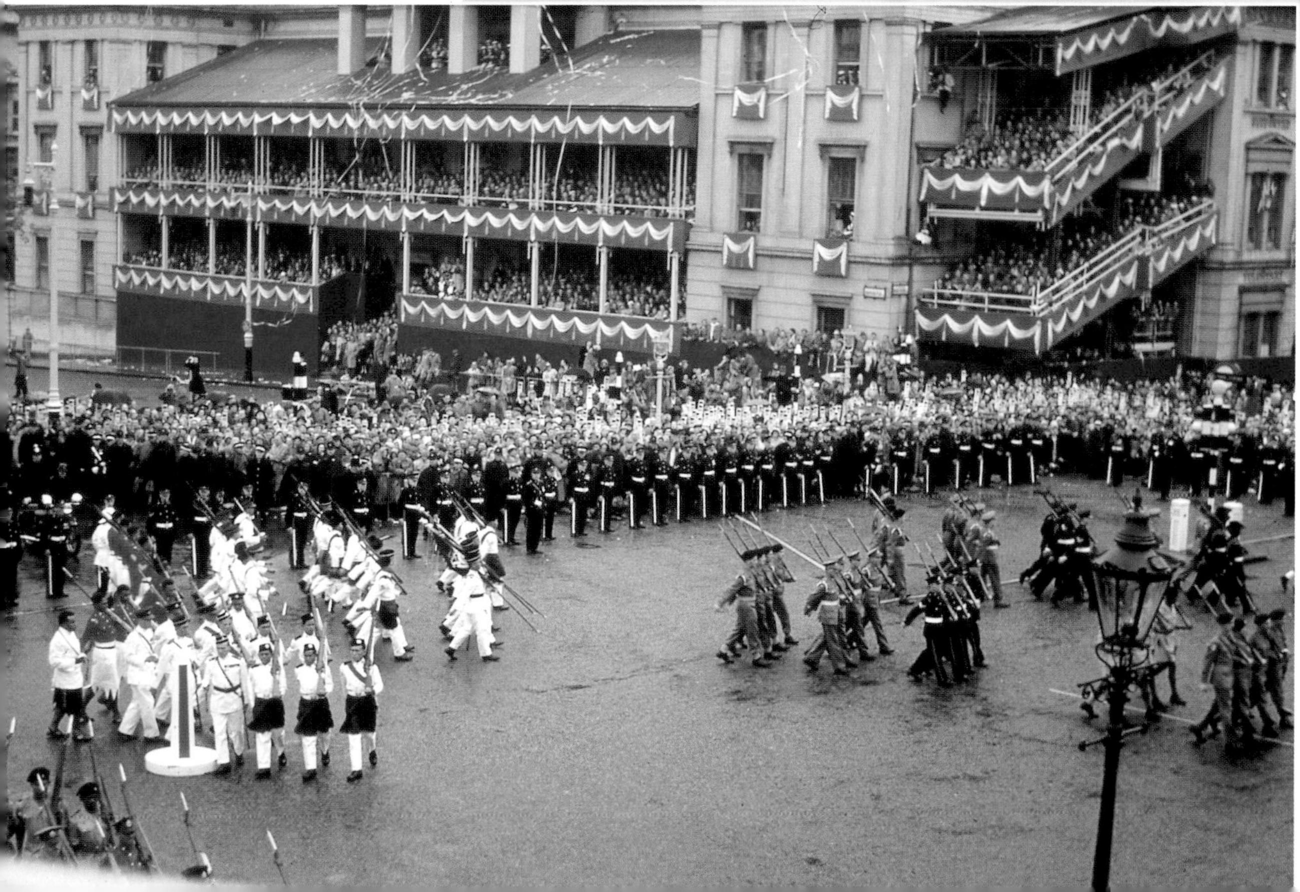

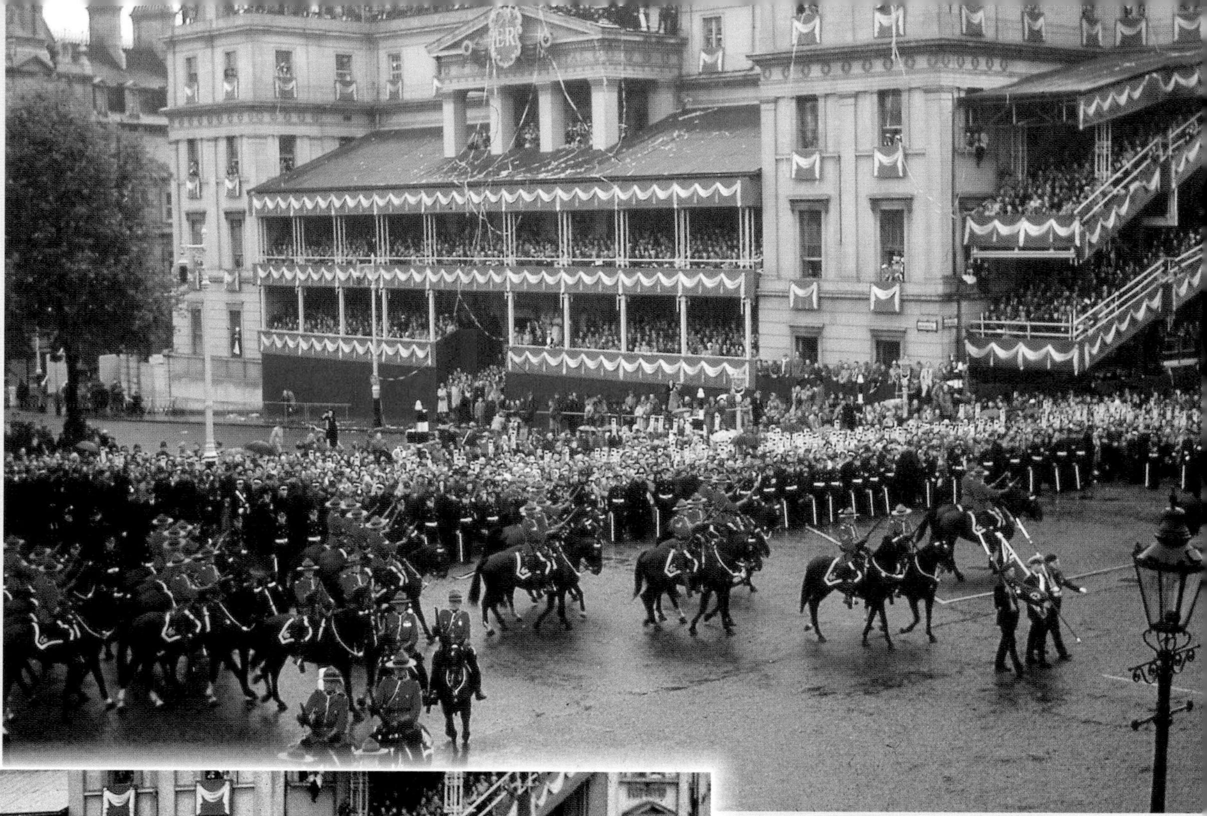

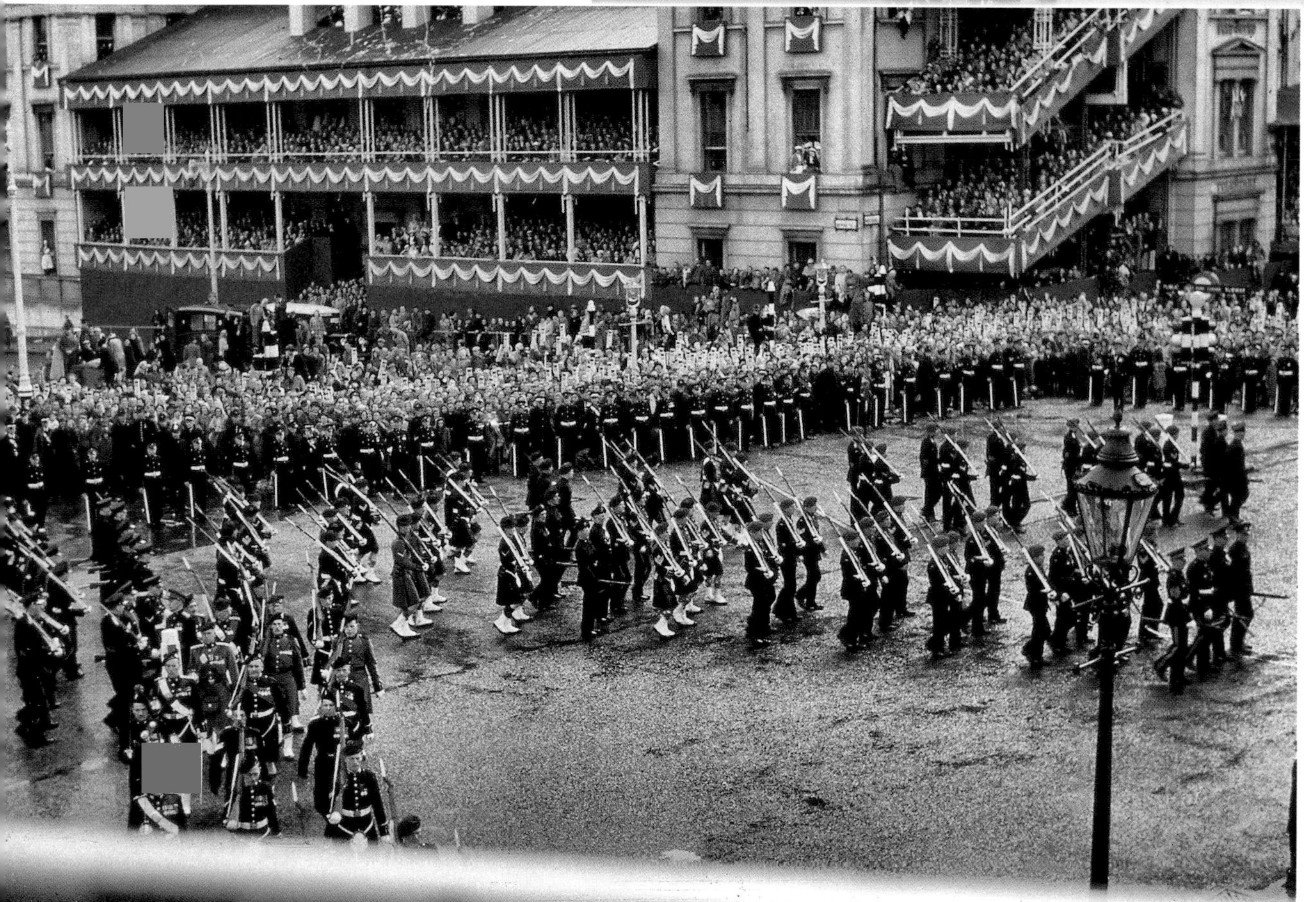

What they came for: a glimpse of gold and magic.

FINALE

The Queen's Coronation Day Speech

The following speech was broadcast by Her Majesty the Queen to her subjects in the United Kingdom and the Commonwealth on the evening of Coronation Day, 2 June 1953:

When I spoke to you last, at Christmas, I asked you all, whatever your religion, to pray for me on the day of my coronation – to pray that God would give me wisdom and strength to carry out the promises that I should then be making.

Throughout this memorable day I have been uplifted and sustained by the knowledge that your thoughts and prayers were with me. I have been aware all the time that my peoples, spread far and wide throughout every continent and ocean in the world, were united to support me in the task to which I have now been dedicated with such solemnity.

Many thousands of you came to London from all parts of the Commonwealth and Empire to join in the ceremony, but I have been conscious too of the millions of others who have shared in it by means of wireless or television in their homes. All of you, near or far, have been united in one purpose. It is hard for me to find words in which to tell you of the strength which this knowledge has given me.

The ceremonies you have seen today are ancient, and some of their origins are veiled in the mists of the past. But their spirit and their meaning shine through the ages never, perhaps, more brightly than now. I have in sincerity pledged myself to your service, as so many of you are pledged to mine. Throughout all my life and with all my heart I shall strive to be worthy of your trust.

In this resolve I have my husband to support me. He shares all my ideals and all my affection for you. Then, although my experience is so short and my task so new, I have in my parents and grandparents an example which I can follow with certainty and with confidence.

There is also this. I have behind me not only the splendid traditions and the annals of more than a thousand years but the living strength and majesty of the Commonwealth and Empire; of societies old and new; of lands and races different in history and origins but all, by God's Will, united in spirit and in aim.

Therefore I am sure that this, my coronation, is not the symbol of a power and a splendour that are gone but a declaration of our hopes for the future, and for the years I may, by God's Grace and Mercy, be given to reign and serve you as your queen.

I have been speaking of the vast regions and varied peoples to whom I owe my duty but there has also sprung from our island home a theme of social and political thought which constitutes our message to the world and through the changing generations has found acceptance both within and far beyond my realms.

Parliamentary institutions, with their free speech and respect for the rights of minorities, and the inspiration of a broad tolerance in thought and expression – all this we conceive to be a precious part of our way of life and outlook.

During recent centuries, this message has been sustained and invigorated by the immense contribution, in language, literature, and action, of the nations of our Commonwealth overseas. It gives expression, as I pray it always will, to living principles, as sacred to the Crown and Monarchy as to its many Parliaments and Peoples. I ask you now to cherish them – and practise them too; then we can go forward together in peace, seeking justice and freedom for all men.

As this day draws to its close, I know that my abiding memory of it will be, not only the solemnity and beauty of the ceremony, but the inspiration of your loyalty and affection. I thank you all from a full heart. God bless you all.

Appendix

❦ THE QUEEN'S BEASTS ❦

As we saw in Chapter 4 a series of ten giant heraldic beasts were produced by the artist James Woodford (1893–1976) to enhance the surroundings of the prefabricated annex to Westminster Abbey. Sadly they are now all but forgotten, a regrettable oversight as they are one of the few pieces of decoration to have survived from the astonishing theatrical set piece which was created in and around the abbey.

Their survival was by no means guaranteed, however, as the ten were rendered by the artist in partially painted plaster, suggesting they were never meant as anything more than temporary set-dressing. The ten are nevertheless exceptionally handsome beasts and deeply symbolic, each of the precious survivors having been chosen to represent a significant part of Her Majesty's realm or – as described below – a component of her rich royal ancestry.

Fortunately following their removal from the abbey annex, and a brief period on public display at two of the historic royal palaces, a decision was taken to preserve them permanently at the Canadian Museum of Civilisation in Gatineau, Quebec. Equally happily, at around the same time, a set of replicas was created – this time in Portland stone – and these can still be seen outside Decimus Burton's splendidly Victorian Palm House at Kew in south-west London.

THE LION OF ENGLAND

The lion has been England's principal royal beast since the twelfth century. For this reason the lion carries the current Royal Arms of the United Kingdom and is the only one of the ten beasts to be depicted wearing a crown.

THE SCOTTISH UNICORN

This unicorn holds a shield of the Royal Arms of Scotland, which readers will recognise from the second quarter of the Royal Arms of the United

Magnificent and mysterious.

Kingdom. Following the death in 1603 of Queen Elizabeth I, and the end of the reign of the House of Tudor, the accession of the Stuarts brought James VI of Scotland to the throne of England as James I. The unicorn thus became the left-hand or sinister supporter of his Royal Arms.

THE FALCON OF THE PLANTAGENETS

Marking the supremacy of a new royal house in 1480, Edward IV gave the surname Plantagenet to his illegitimate son, Arthur Viscount Lisle. The emblems of the falcon and a fetterlock – a device for hobbling horses – were used by both the Yorkist and Lancastrian descendants of Edward III.

THE GOLDEN GRIFFIN OF EDWARD III

Appearing on Edward's seal, the Griffin was depicted by Woodford holding the newest royal badge, that of the House of Windsor. During the First World War, in 1917, George V had adopted the more obviously English name for his family. His son, George VI, authorised the use of the new badge from 1938 onwards, the image on it representing the Round Tower at Windsor Castle flying the Royal Banner and surrounded by oak leaves.

THE WHITE LION OF MORTIMER

A favourite of Edward IV, the uncrowned lion bears a shield of Yorkist colours (blue and mulberry) with a white rose and white lion badge inherited from his grandmother, Anne de Mortimer, Countess of Cambridge.

THE WHITE GREYHOUND OF RICHMOND

The greyhound traditionally bears a shield of Tudor colours (white and green) with a Tudor rose surmounted by a crown. Henry VII, the Tudors' dynastic founder, sometimes flew greyhounds on his standard and used them as supporters on his coat of arms. Combining the red rose of Lancaster and the Yorkists' white rose the Tudor rose underlines the successful union of the warring parties.

THE BLACK BULL OF CLARENCE

Such animals provided the supporters of the arms of the Duke of Clarence, Edward III's third son and the person from who the Yorkist kings descend. Woodford's bull bears a shield containing the Royal Arms of England. It is shown in the form used between 1405 and 1603, that is to say one which indicates the country's longstanding claim to the throne of France.

THE SILVER YALE OF BEAUFORT

With the body of an antelope or goat, a lion's tail, and a head mounted with boar's tusks and swivelling horns, the mythical yale is associated with Lady Margaret Beaufort, the mother of the Lancastrian Henry VII. The first Tudor king ascended to the throne of England in 1485, following the death of Richard III and a year before his marriage to Elizabeth of York united the Houses of York and Lancaster.

THE RED DRAGON OF CADWALLADER

In various guises the dragon appears in Welsh chronicles from the sixth century onwards, prompting Sir Owen Tudor (grandfather to Henry VII) to adopt it as his personal symbol when he began to claim descent from Cadwallader, last native king of Britain. Through such cynical manipulation of history he sought to benefit from a prophecy that a Cadwallader descendant would one day rule England.

THE WHITE HORSE OF HANOVER

The most recent arrival in the British royal menagerie, Woodford's White Horse holds a shield bearing the Royal Arms of the United Kingdom. They appear in the form used from 1714 until 1801, that is to say following the accession of the Elector of Hanover as George I when the Electorate's white horse – a potent Saxon symbol – was incorporated into the fourth quarter of the Royal Arms.

If you enjoyed this book, you may also be interested in…

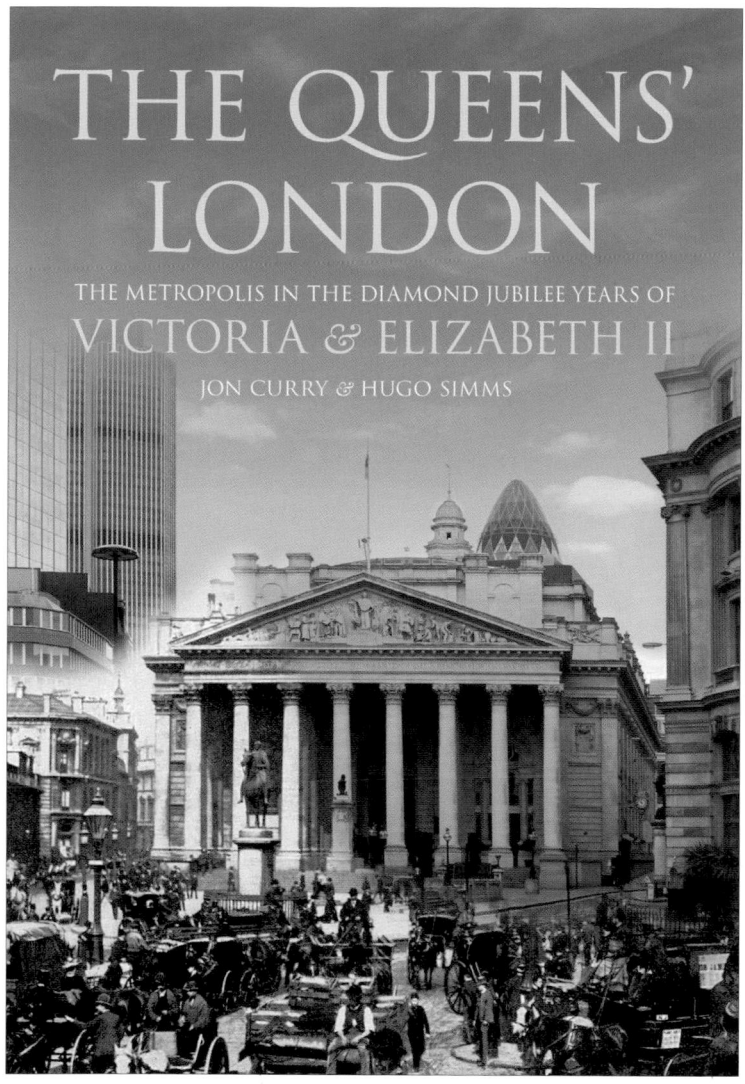

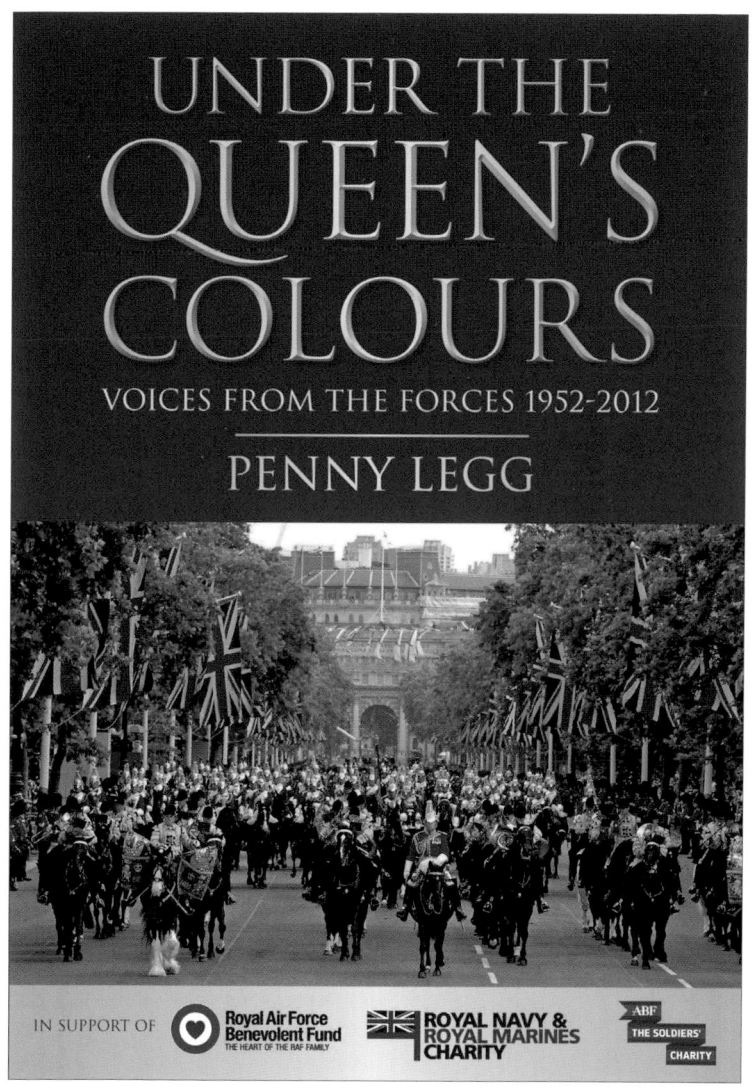

The Queens' London
9780752470115

Under the Queen's Colours
9780752469959

If you enjoyed this book, you may also be interested in…

The Coronation: A Royal History
9781841654218

The Queen's Coronation Day
9781841654003